Bloom

Copyright © 2021 by Red Penguin Books

Editor Nika Jordan Rose

All rights reserved

Published by Red Penguin Books

Bellerose Village, New York

ISBN

Print 978-1-63777-027-6

Digital 978-1-63777-026-9

No part of this volume may be reproduced in any form or by any electronic or mechanical means, including information storage and retrieval systems, without written permission from the author, except for the use of brief quotations in a book review.

## CONTACT US

For general inquiries, write to
bloomlitmagazine@gmail.com

## SUBMISSIONS

If you'd like to contribute, email us at
bloomlitmagazine@gmail.com

## SPONSORS

To enquire about advertising or sponsorships,
get in touch at stephanie@redpenguinbooks.com

## CONTRIBUTORS

Maddie Anderlik
Helen Aitchison
Mark Blickley
Romi Cruanas
Debbie De Louise
Jean Ende
Eran E. Eads
Jack M. Freedman
Samantha Funk
Beaton Galafa
Howie Good
Giles Robert Goodland
Elana Gomel
Shannon Frost Greenstein
John Grey
Westley Heine
June Hunter
Trish Lindsey Jaggers
Dan Keeble
Katie Keridan

John Lambremont, Sr.
Joesph S Mannino
Ben Macnair
Thomas M. McDade
Alaina Messineo
Amanda Montoni
Guna Moran
Christy O'Callaghan
Audrey Rauth
Lisa Rosenblatt
William John Rostron
Tali Cohen Shabtai
Victoria Tracy
Jim Tritten
Marlene Tully
Antonio Vallone
A.O. Wallat
Robert Wynne
Jenna Zeihen

No part of this publication may be reproduced, distributed, or transmitted in any form or by any means, including photocopying, or other electronic or mechanical methods, without the prior written permission of the editor.

# from the editor...

Welcome to *Bloom*, the literary magazine dedicated to the growth of the emerging (or re-emerging) author! We are delighted to share our first issue with you. In the pages ahead you will find work by writers, both emerging and established, that pushes against limitations of form, content, and style. It is our hope that *Bloom* will continue to act as a virtual "playground" for writers to explore their work without restriction, try their hand at something new, and/or finally submit that piece they thought couldn't quite "fit" in traditional publishing. As I sifted through the over 300 submissions we received for this issue, I was ecstatic with the variance in pieces. From the sacred to the experimental, our call for exciting original work was truly met! I hope that you read through this issue with intention and leave with a fire burning within you to write something new, something you never thought you would or could write, something that expands you, and most importantly, leads to growth as an author. We look forward to seeing that work in our next edition. Until then, enjoy the beautiful chaos!

*Nika Rose*

*an interv*
*rawlings*

USA Today Bestselling Author Rachel Rawlings was born and raised in the Baltimore Metropolitan area and has always had a fascination with the strange and unusual. Although her passion for writing developed early on, it wasn't until 2009 that she published her first novel - to prove a point to her children. When she isn't writing Urban Fantasy or Paranormal Romance, Rachel can be found with her nose buried in a good book and a cup of coffee nearby. There may or may not be cookies!

Rachel Rawlings USA Today Bestselling Author of Paranormal Romance and Urban Fantasy
http://www.rachelrawlings.com/
www.facebook.com/RachelRawlingsAuthor
Twitter: @rachelsbooks
Instagram: @rachelsbook

# an interview with rachel rawlings
# by bloom editor nika rose

NIKA: Let's start at the beginning. Can you tell me a bit about how and when you started writing?

RACHEL: I've always written; finishing writing was something different. I was always kind of scribbling story openers or a couple of chapters, a lot of poetry through middle and high school, but I didn't really finish anything until late 2009, and then really more with publishing in 2010. But it was really more like, I had this idea in my head, and I would email a few chapters to a friend of mine, and with each email it got longer and longer and longer, and then next thing you know it's a book. At the very beginning with indie publishing, as I was kind of "coming up" with KPD, I just thought "y'know, why not?" At least I can say I did it, and have a book I can show my kids, like "you can still do it, it doesn't have to be huge" and I wasn't expecting best sellers of anything like that, it was really more about accomplishing this task, setting this goal for myself, and with my kids. "If you can dream it you can do it." And then, a dozen or so books later, here we are. And it's a completely different thing than what I thought. I've worked full-time jobs and ran small businesses in between and still published. We just moved halfway across the country last year, so there's always these life changes that you can't predict, but writing has always been a staple.

N: Do you still do other things for work or has writing become your full-time career?

R: This is my mostly full-time now. I also do author services, providing support to other authors, whether it's marketing support, personal assisting, virtual assisting support. Taking what I've learned as an author myself–and the running "Hallowread" for several years, which was a book festival–and just what I've learned from courses, I just throw that expertise out there for them to benefit from. Because it's hard to be able to do everything. And that's just since we moved out to Tennessee. Prior to that, I was working, running the family business for years. We had two salons out in Ellicott City, Maryland, one in Ellicott City, one in Havre de Grace. And then we lost the one in Ellicott City the day after the flood. The second floor was just too much, after two huge flash floods eighteen months apart, coming back from the second one was… I don't know, I'm proud of my friends in town who did it, but for us being in the service industry, it's really hard to know if you're going to have people in there, like does that make you culpable if it happens again. We were just emotionally exhausted. And then I moved. The universe throws these things at you, and everything is meant to work out. So that kind of opened things up. It was like "we're moving" and then you're like "well, what do you do" and I thought "Oh, well I can take all of the stuff that I've learned and make a new career." So still writing, and then being able to work with authors, and make a career out of that as well has been pretty cool.

N: Can you tell me a little about your fixation with the paranormal? What drew you to that realm?

R: I'm like Lydia Deets–"I myself am strange and unusual". My gosh. The first books I really vividly remember reading were those "Choose Your Own Adventure" books. I loved those. And there was always the one that had… it was a princess, and I can't remember all the specifics, but she was the hero of her own story and it had like elves and different stuff, so there's always been this kind of fantasy… And then after that,

I remember watching Legend, the first movie I saw in theatres, or remember seeing in the theatres, there was The Last Unicorn and then there was Legend so I feel like it's always been a thing for me.

N: Do you think the paranormal genre has something to offer our culture at this particular moment in time?

R: It provides a great escape. If you're looking for an escape, a dystopian novel might not be where you want to go. Sometimes it feels like we're in a sci-fi novel, and I love those genres too. But I think, and I don't know, some people might say it's a horrorshow, some people might not want to read horror right now, but I do think they provide an escape. Because you're not going to go outside and find a werewolf in your front yard… although, after 2020, I'm not ruling anything out at this point, but really theoretically speaking, it should be being able to slip into a fantasy. Especially with urban fantasy where you have that "right now" of the modern setting, but at least we know we're probably not going to find a vampire roaming the streets.

N: I've heard you mention both "urban fantasy" and "paranormal romance" as words to describe your writing. Could you tell me a little more about what those terms mean to you?

R: They're pretty common bedfellows, I think. The main difference is, urban fantasy can definitely have romance, but if you pull the romance out of the story altogether does the plot still hold? It's a little more action-driven or problem-solving driven with urban fantasy. The romance can be there but it's usually a subplot, not the main plot. Where, with paranormal romance, it tends to be the focus. If you took the romance out it would be, well, you'd still kind of have a plot but it wouldn't hold the book together. So the biggest difference is what is holding your plot threads together.

N: You mentioned the Hallowread festival, can we talk about how that came to fruition?

R: That was a lovechild. I'd done a lot of book events, had done some big ones out of New York and Chicago, that were comic-related. And they're very open to authors, obviously, but they're more pop culture cons now than they are strictly comic conventions. And the book-related ones were always welcoming, they're not "exclusive," but they were centered around romance, more traditional romance, at least at the time I was starting Hallowread. And I thought, well there's so many of us that have romance, but it's not that "bread-and-butter" romance people are used to. I didn't have topless guys on my covers, there were no glistening pecs and abs. I just felt like I wasn't what the attendees were expecting. Listen, romance is still the number one genre, it sells and there's no denying it. I'm not knocking anybody, put those abs on there! There's a reader for that! But I also thought, there are readers for genre fiction too, and they may not be going to these particular festivals I was at because they weren't looking for, primarily, contemporary romance. Whether they were looking for something more steampunk or thriller… And readers, a lot of them don't pigeonhole themselves. I tend to stick to the same things, I'm a creature of habit. But some of my author friends are expanding my tastes with contemporary romance, you read something that someone's written in like an author support group and I'm like "Oh, I didn't think I liked contemporary romance but you've brought me over! I'm stepping out of the darkside." But you have to find your community and I think that was the biggest thing for Hallowread. I thought, let's give it a whirl, and I reached out to an events committee and I said "I have this crazy idea, bear with me. It's not going to have any beer. It's not going to have any bands. It's going to be books!" And they were receptive. And I wanted to do it around Halloween and theme it all around that. And they were totally down for it, which blew my mind because it's so nerdy. I didn't think it would sell with an events committee that does primarily music events and beer gardens. And here I am, "We're going to have books!" We ran it seven years, had some awesome keynote speakers come out, and made connections with authors and readers. I was always kind of like Charlie Bucket. I was just super glad to be there. It was either feeling like Charlie or that you're a parent that planned a birthday party for your kid and you're worried about whether people will show up. It was two warring emotions. Everything leading up to the day was nervous parent energy and then the day of "wow, people came, I can't believe it!" And you're just super grateful. It was so great, and then you're like "how do I top that"? Last year was our big grand finale. It's so hard to let go of something that was such a huge part of my life. But moving to Tennessee made it a really hard part of my life–to move back to Maryland and coordinate everything–because you work on it all year round, it's not just in September leading up to October. You're planning one year and you're still looking ahead to the next year trying to book people, it was a never-ending cycle. So I had to say goodbye, it was devastating.

N: I'm circling back a bit here, but could you talk a little bit about your personal writing process? How do you start a new project or develop one that you've been working on?

R: Being a writer is kind of like having multiple personality disorder, and everyone is fighting for attention at the same time. I have post-it notes on my laptop with all kinds of ideas. I have one for the paranormal I want to write, another three-book series, etc. Right now I probably have seven "to-be-writtens", and I know authors with even more than that, three or four times more than that. I think it comes down to which voice becomes the loudest, and that's the one you have to give your attention to. For me, my process… we're early risers, my husband has been in assembly forever so he's first-shift. I get up with him, we're up at 3:00, he's out the door by 4:30 and I'm prepping to write. 4:30-5:00 I may be going through emails, checking up with whatever my client work is going to be for the day. 5:00-6:30 it's writing and copious amounts of coffee. After that it's getting the kids ready, everybody up and ready for the day. I sprint more than anything else, it's really writing sprints every day and before you know it it's off to the editor. Maybe not before you know it, I'm not as fast as some people. Which is okay. I'm learning it's a process, I'm a work in process—I try not to compare myself to other people. That would be my biggest piece of advice too, to anyone writing–don't compare your process to someone else's, because it's so individual, so personal, the whole writing experience. One of my friends is a savant. If she sits down to write, she can crank out a book that's like 75,000-80,000 words in two weeks. And I can't do that in two months! It's personal, what we choose to do or how our days work out, or how our minds work. I'm working on it every day. I encourage everyone to do the same, not to compare your process to someone else's. Write that book that you feel needs to be written, at the time, for you.

N: At what point in your writing journey did you start to bring other people onto your team (editors, agents, etc)? Did you self-publish first?

R: I think it was by my third book that I became more aware of the resources available to self-publishers and not just to traditional authors. I learned that there were editors and cover artists that freelanced, that did work outside of "the big five". Then it was a matter of going back and fixing your earlier work later in your career, because it's a growth process. Where you are at book twelve probably isn't where you were at book one. So you have these editors that you work with or these cover artists and you may want to go back and revisit old projects. Because I got in so early and didn't really intend on making a career out of it, or have any longevity doing it at all, and I thought it was just going to be that one book. Then I had the second book and there was more to tell and I had more ideas and you think "okay, there have to be people out there that are doing the same thing I am but just a different line of work, within this work, and how do I find them?" Now, they're everywhere, the resources are astounding. Being able to find editors and artists and writing groups where authors support each other, it's amazing. That was the craziest thing about Hallowread too, even locally in Marymount, we had so many authors coming from Maryland, and I thought "how are you all coming from the same state as me?" How is this a thing that there's this many of us in one little state"? And it's like that everywhere you move, it's "how is it possible there are this many creatives?" but there are. And it's a pretty awesome community.

N: Last question. I'm just curious, and maybe the answer is "it hasn't", but how do you feel the pandemic has changed the way you approach writing?

R: It's definitely affected my motivation, or maybe my output. I mean the world is on fire literally and figuratively and that has an impact. I've always been a person who reads the news–my husband and I do that together every morning when we get up. Maybe I should take a hiatus from that. Some people unplug from social media, but that's kind of part of my world as an author and also as a support person to other authors. I can't really unplug from that. I try to spend as little time on Twitter as possible—I jump in, make a post, and I'm out. It's such a rapid-fire system that you can see stuff when you're really trying to tune out. I should probably do that with the news for a couple of days and see if that does anything. It gets hard. Even when you're writing fiction and it's witches and vampires, whatever it is. It can still be hard to feel positivity within your creativity when everything around you seems to be kind of negative. That's probably the biggest thing. It hasn't impacted my content so much, that's been pretty consistent, but definitely my output, my flow, isn't as good.

N: There's been a lot of discourse across fields about working under these new conditions and, while it might seem like writers would be less affected since you typically work from now, but it still takes a toll on your creative faculties.

R: You're right about that part; it hasn't been an adjustment in workspace. It's weird having other people home, in my workspace, so that has been an adjustment. If I had spare time, maybe I could fluctuate my schedule with my assistant work, maybe I could take lunch now, maybe I could do something for myself, maybe I'm working on an audiobook, a contract for that or something else. Now I'm working on math. So there's been an adjustment there, too. You're mentally exhausted from being in sixth grade for eight hours a day. Sometimes I get up and all I can think about is dividing decimals and fractions, whatever happened the day before and I have to think, "now what was I writing about in that last chapter"? It is different. We're all making adjustments. I'm happy to do it, I feel like it's the bare minimum I can do. But I think we're all ready for a bit of normal.

N: Thank you so much for talking to me!

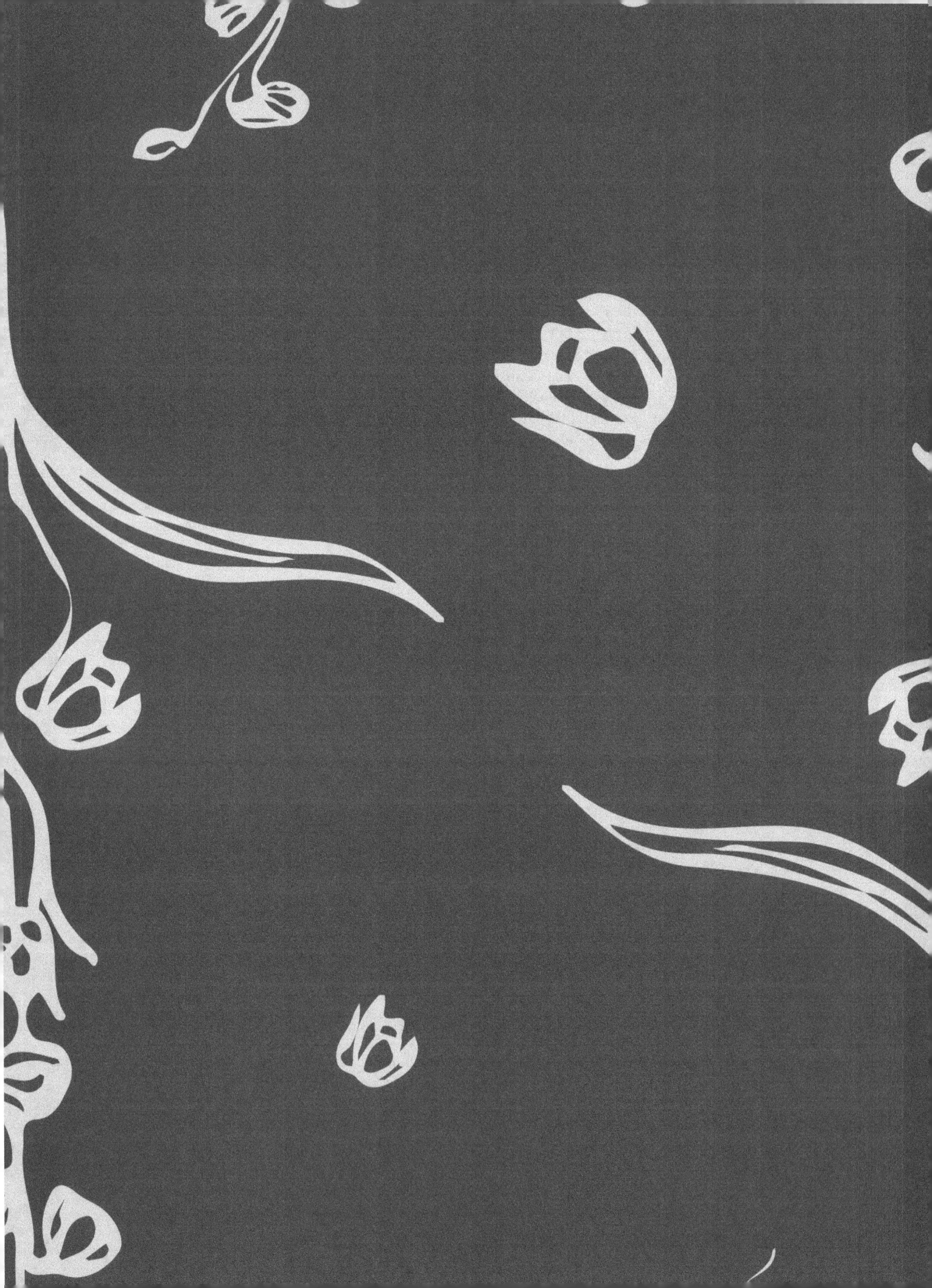

## My Dream in the Garden
## Jenna Zeihen

Maybe you've wept there too.
Wrapped in blankets from before-
Before you knew this feeling.
Before you felt your absence,
 More Often,
Than your presence.
The pictures on the bedroom walls
Have faded now,
A memory run out of time.
My ghost lives here.
Who knew our thoughts expired-
I see her too.
When I dream, I don't know I am dreaming.
Does that mean this is a dream?
Clocks running faster than they used to,
I can't see as clearly-
But oh I can feel much more.
Are the blind closer to heaven?
I'm running through the garden in my dreams.
Looking for something,
Looking for you.
Soft white light.
Somewhere between the hard and soft.
Nothing would be more empty,
Than us poured together-
Yet running dry.
You overflow all on your own.
We collide gently.
You have shown me more of me than any
Mirror
Or shadow
Or photograph
Could ever see.

**Dizzy With Infinity**
**J.S. Mannino**

Let's illuminate the abstract
Transcend a quantum leap
Reality skews the ether
Light permeates the deep

Where one thread ends
Another spins free
Looping back onto itself
Dizzy with infinity

The signal breaks down
Closer to the source
The patterns that emerge
Circumscribes a subtle force

Waves parse dark matter
Fractals bloom in proximity
Light stalls at the event horizon
Dizzy with infinity

Deeper towards the bottom
Reality comes apart
Strings pulse with information
The source code for the start

All matter coalesces
Elegant in simplicity
Staring at the origin
Dizzy with infinity

**Anachronome**
**J.S. Mannino**

Hardwired to our source code
Subconsciously prepared
Transmitted by antenna
To the mind yet unimpaired

Anxious wires vibrating
Growing accordant buzz
Alternating progressions
To transcend the cosmic fuzz

Keys surge in synthesis
Sounds in varied degrees
Ambient landscapes of mood
Born of nuanced subtleties

Vibrating cables pulse
Crunchy metallic thrum
Synchronizes our heartbeats
With every subsequent strum

Rhythmic thunder crashing
Percussive tribal forms
Turns those cardiac events
Into surging sonic storms

Static on the airwaves
Noises from the abstract
Oscillating frequencies
Built for maximum impact

The arrangement plays on
In aching earnest bliss
Harmonious sounds engage
Through the crackling hollow hiss

Simplicity of song
Though elegant in rhyme
Finds beauty from the chaos
Of music that transcends time

## Haiku For Autumn
## John Lambermont

autumn comes quickly
one lonely firefly flashing
final green warning


white men in gray clothes
statues for a summertime
hands still pointing south


orange sunshine pool
winged bubbles drift aimlessly
air of an evening


man-made slabs of white
celebration of falling
nature confetti


rainy night sojourn
red street lights never beacons
violent reminders


sung in a song once
jellyfish float in gray water
red cork bobbing still

## The Ballerina
## Amanda Montoni

There was a ballerina in Central Park today. She wore pink:
pink tights, pink leotard, pink tutu, pink shoes. I saw her from the terrace.

People stopped to look at her grace, her poise,
but most of all,
her astonishing ability to fly.

She was a swan
next to the bronze fountain.
Her long body complimented the lake behind her. Her pink softness
clashed with the hard red brick against her feet. Her beauteous wings glistened in the
sunlight like diamonds.

She stood on her toes, never lost her balance, and flew.
She flew.

She was in a place of tranquility we only dream of.

For a few moments,
all the worrying stopped.
For a few moments,
the hustle of the city stopped. For a few moments,
the whole world stopped.

I walked down the terrace steps to the fountain, took a coin out of my purse, closed my eyes,
and threw to coin

to join the other forgotten wishes in the shimmering metal water.

I wished I could fly.
Fly far away from this place like the ballerina.

I snapped a picture
and headed back to work.
When I got home,
my mother asked me what happened that day. I showed her the picture and she said "It looks like she's flying."

There was a ballerina in Central Park today.

## *september*
### Victoria Tracy

Sun-bleached stairs are creaking / gusts of wind continue swelling outside the shattered windows / Heavy drops are bouncing across the tin roof / forgotten ghosts of past lovers are camping in the cluttered attic/

This house is a paper mache shelter / succumbing, slowly, to mother's unrelenting rage / but i am unscathed/

Here, in your arms / my fingers are trekking across the forbidden trails of your damp frame / no storm can reach us / we are clasped together / heaving chests / slick with summer heat/

Sweet humidity is humming her gently melody / the muggy tune drifts in dreamy patterns across our ears / southern nights like this are wrapped in sweet red wine / we are tied together with mosquito kisses and cicada handshakes /

It is hotter than the damned devil's mansion / thick air fills your lung like molasses / god is playing his drums too loudly in the background /

Nightfall is glittering as lightning bugs tend to their weekly errands / the wicker loveseat is leaving indentations on your exposed thighs / citronella taines the heavy air/

The surge moves on / leaving our wretched souls to rummage through the wreckage / collapsed memories litter the sand / but you are still holding my hand //

**friendship**
**Sam Funk**

he sits facing towards her on the back of the patio
she swirls her black straw until the ice taps the side of the plastic cup;
a nervous habit—one they both recognize.

the only ones at this relatively abandoned bagel shop
they speak freely of politics and their hunger for a world of empathy;
as tea touches her dry lips she begins to remember what lights her fire again.

for the last few months in the summer heat everything has been ice cold
her dreary heart miles away from natural joy;
they munch on bagels with lox.

while the hum of the tiny birds in the busy city lays quietly above them
she is no longer afraid to take the risks she once was;
for she is certain that there is nobody else in the world that could convince her to eat raw tomatoes
and actually like them.

the potted plants lie above on the backdrop behind him
and the familiar sound of take-out paper bags crinkle in moments of comfortable silence;
when she speaks of nonsensical family traditions and tries to make them palpable.

## love
### Sam Funk

leaves touch the bottom of her rubber boots
the same ones she wore last winter;
when he saw her become herself once again.

skipping in the creek and by the rocks near the waterfall
he watches her with glee;
his happiness no doubt, often contingent on hers.

ice cream on a park bench
the sun rests behind her golden hair;
and he looks at her as if he is just as in awe of her as in the beginning.

of course she notices the look
but says nothing;
for it's a look they both frequent, in exchange with each other.

the love of daily tasks
of missing each other when gone for just the day;
she is certain her love is just as passionate as it is—boring.

# The Accidents that Aren't
## Shannon Frost Greenstein

How many times
do we avoid catastrophe
by an inch,
a blink, a heartbeat, a nanosecond that passes in an instant and still holds
the entire world in the span of its
breathless life
*safety as illusion, safety as naivete, safety as scrim between the sides of the veil*
*safety as Oz the Great and Terrible behind his curtain, safety as sure as the random roll of the dice, safety*
*as placeholder, because we are all waiting*

How many near-misses,
the cars we usher ahead of us and patches of ice we miss and shoelaces on which we never trip
*God a puppet-master and we are marionettes, strings knotted, limbs akimbo, walk-ons in the Book of Job.*
*We are all waiting.*
How often do we court death,
blissfully unaware?

The Accidents that Aren't
haunt me
*anxiety like magma simmering boiling erupting through my limbic system*
*compulsions and obsessions and the Sword of Damocles always*
*hanging*
even though I am ignorant that they
even exist even though nothing has even existed
to exist at all;
legion, for they are many,
and sometimes I see them
beckoning
like *l'appel du vide*, and we are all waiting.

I am safe
now
from the Accidents that Turned Out Never to Be.
Tomorrow?
Safety as sanctuary
from The Call of the Void
while we all wait.

## When the Cloud Descends
## Shannon Frost Greenstein

It falls, a storm,
silent suffering condensed into
weeping droplets,
precipitates of pain hanging like a pall,
a Sword of Damocles
swinging between endurance and
respite and
life and
death
when the cloud descends.

The world seems good
better
my family seems good
better
the future seems good
better
without me –
without my failure, without my weakness, without my ineptitude and influence and illness and damage –
when the cloud descends.

Time stretches like
taffy, living experience swallowed by
a fog of unrest.
Life continues and
I continue,
the best I can,
never enough,
when the cloud descends.

Then
a moment
of illumination, a rogue photon, a shadow
through the rage and
disgust and frustration and fear,
the light splinters through
the scrim of the squall
refracting into brilliant colors, a bright spectrum of emotion
at last

I survive again and
I will be filled with gratitude and joy –
motherhood, coffee, orgasms, cats, dopamine, love –
until the next time, and the next, and the next
when the cloud descends.

# A SHY MAN AT THE CLUB
## John Grey

If nothing happens tonight,
I will imagine I am yet to be.
Or I've arrived. And I've left.

I sit by the speakers,
by the electric guitar loneliness,
sound, gossip from the next table,
waitress, drinks on a tray:
I am surrounded by many horizons.

But if tonight is like every other night,
my intentions will not be met.
I'll have to step back two hundred years.
Or lurch forward a thousand.

A young woman trails her girlfriend to the bathroom.
Another is at one with the taste of
the green concoction she sips.
A third is dancing with the handsome devil.
A fourth sits alone, but I can't bring myself to ask,
Have you no mother, no lover, no unfulfilled desire?
She is so calm. Why don't her fingers tap?
I have so much love? Has she equal amounts of farewell?

But no levers are pulled. No double lines are jumped.
Roads can't join together, when the woman and I
know only how to walk them singly.

The music pummels on.
The conversation likewise.
I sit in ironclad silence.
She gets up to leave.
Without me.
My heart's never traveled in glad leaps.
And hers has never waited up for someone.

Back at my table,
two of life's discordant prospects
occupy one frame:
I'm yet to arrive. I'm long gone.
I am dead. I am not yet born.
I am in my life, that boundary
of every other life.

## LIFE IN THE CITY
### John Grey

crowd at the farmer's market -
I run my fingers over a home-made bowl -
I love its scars,
the seminal spots where smoothness ends -
if only touch could speak
but the potter's talking to her German shepherd;


the film is French.
attracts only the scattered few -
on the screen,
the faces of the audience,
even the palms of my hands -
I see sub-titles everywhere;


my apartment building
knows how to keep
a boiler-maker and a ballerina apart -
it uses numbers on doors -
it applies walls and ceiling -
even the like-minded
can't wrap their brains around the fact
that elevators are designed
to stop at different floors;


in the park,
only pigeons come to be fed;
at the office,
cubicles stand guard over conversation;
a club provides noise
and freelancers
who are never what they say they are;
add up all the occasional one-stand stands
and the answer is always
one very long and dissipated evening;


I sit in my room
and look down, stare up -
windows and strangers, traffic and stars -
just because a place is populated
doesn't mean there is someone.

# THE OLYMPICS
## John Grey

Sure I get weepy
watching all the nations
on the planet
marching around in a ring.

There's everybody from the
fastest runners
to the swiftest swimmers
and the men and women
who can toss a discus
farther than I can chase a chicken.
And a flame is lit.
I'm a sucker for a flame being lit.

And it all goes back
to ancient Greece
with a slight intermission
of two thousand years ago.

There's no contest
for who can recite
Gray's Elegy Written In A Country Churchyard
without messing up a line.

No, this is all about bodies.
Some muscular, some lithe,
but all with sinew suitable to their sport.
They do smile
but only when medals are hung from their throats,
not because they've just read Molly Bloom's soliloquy.

The commentators gush.
Why shouldn't they? I do.
And this is only the opening ceremony.
The athletes endear themselves to me
just by showing up.
Here's some guy from a country
that has never even come close to winning a medal.
His homeland is at war so I'm informed.
Now there's a sport that the Olympics
needs to add to its schedule.
Countries like his would finally get their due.
And you could be dead and still medal.

## HE WAS A FRIEND
## John Grey

I can admit that now
but not then.
I can look in the mirror,
say, "Repeat after me,
he was a friend."
But, when I knew him,
either there were no mirrors
or I just didn't like
to give myself orders.
Yes, he cheated,
he stole from me,
would have sold my soul
to the devil
were old Nick ever to deal with proxies.
Each one of my
potential girlfriends
became his in actuality.
And, as for that job
that should have been mine,
he lied his way into it.
We were roommates
but extracting his share of the rent money
required something close to fracking.
And don't get me started on his drunken binges
or the time he stuffed the telltale drugs
in the pocket of my jacket.
He was the one friend
that I have to say
I well and truly hated.
Given a more violent disposition
I would have kicked him down the stairs.
But he was the one,
among all of my friends,
who taught me to just
sit and take it
if I wanted the friendship to survive.
I haven't seen him in twenty years.
Nor will I ever again.
His obituary photo stunned me.
It looked worse than a Botox calamity.
So I confess he was a friend of mine.
Otherwise, who else
am I supposed to mourn.

### Green Genes
### Jack m. Freedman

Daybreak illuminates orchards
Apples unable to reproduce

Trees grow amid bloodshed
Leaves stripped to form a demonic pact

Heart abundant
with the devil's delight


Fruits of festering frustration
ripened by ridicule?

Farmers must reach sainthood
after the death of purpose


Purity of their labor
prevailing amid corruption

We as organisms could
modify our own genetics

evolving without
chemical castration

### The First Sign of Spring in Bethlehem, Pennsylvania
### Antonio Vallone

Late March.
Among melting remnants
of the fourth Northeastern winter storm,
an old woman wearing a robin red
tee shirt and Bermuda shorts
sits in a white plastic lawn chair
on her back porch, chain-smoking cigarettes.

As she exhales, plumes
of smoke rise like ranted messages
to the remaining cold.

**Lingering thought**
**Beaton Galafa**

i am an incomplete poem
rolling
to fill the void
grief carves out of
a book page. the grass
and a pile of dead leaves
burning behind my home
speak to the spirits of
my ancestors as they stand
in the night watching
smoke wandering off
to all sides of the earth
in all seasons. they remember
me bending my back
for hours tussling for turf
with leaves from a dying
autumn. without hope,
without sorrow. just
lost in thoughts of
everything about everything
not noticing how trees
survive all seasons to
bear testimony of
winds and fires and rains
that travel through leaving
destruction behind. i am a
poem in writing
rolling itself out to understand
how grief is constant
even with time, always
tucked beneath our eyes
to drop into an expansive sea of
tears any time of the year.

## Migraines
### Beaton Galafa

A deflated body
tossed in mud &
dirty streams
floats side by side
with garbage,
there must come a time
now or in the sweeping of years
when it will stick
to the bottom
& rest.
but that is just that.
migraines will not just
go as they came
until the cavity
in your hugs is filled
with butterflies & flowers
unmanned by strangers
in the twinning of our
sorry lives.

**Empty Bodies**
**Beaton Galafa**

The hissing sound
of my voice
recorded from
a silver-grey phone
on oxygen
blocks a preacher's
noise as his saliva
& sweat from kids
running in these streets
hit the floor, waiting
for rains to flow together
into dying streams
where humanity
on empty tummies
pee & piss their grief
out, not knowing what
to offload from
empty bodies that
at times do not
even carry
homeless souls.

## Rumors about Clouds
### Robert Wynne

On clear days, they gather behind the sun
and conspire to create complementary shapes
like the fish and the bicycle. A wisp of water

forms a stethoscope during thunderstorms,
reaches toward bolts of light, listening.
Even dragon-shaped clouds would admit

there are no such things as dragons,
but fiction can be fun too, which is why
Don Quixote still makes appearances

when windmills spin themselves into being.
The fluffy axe always chases the willowy tree
in vain. No matter how still the sky

clouds witness the wide earth turning
away like a scorned lover, or a god.
Sometimes they cry, but no one can tell

the difference between rain and tears.
The jet stream thinks it's nothing but beer
unleashed across that blue expanse

and searching for a pint glass –
rare in the eye of the beholder.
Whenever an ice cream cone appears

suddenly everything else is a tongue.

## Finally
## Romi Cruanas

Finally first Kisses followed each other
first tongues
first tastes of ashtray in my mouth

I wanted more

it was not enough to kiss one
I wanted to kiss two and three
Even at the same time

I made it, the long awaited first
and now there was no end

I wanted more attention
and less eyes on me
more hands and
more tongues

I thought I was already a woman
while the kid trapped in me
played grown up.

Swimming pool pervs
looking at who I was kissing next.

lust started to smell like freedom
and fear.

## SUN PLEASE DO NOT COME DOWN
### Origin : Assamese : Guna Moran
### Translation : Bibekananda Choudhury

The claimant to the first garland
Is the eternal Sun

But the Sun do not descend to accept the garland

It has to bow down
To wear it
The erudite Sun knows it very well

We spread his fame and virtues
In the absence of the Sun

People garland me
With the one that is meant for the Sun

Once I got it around my neck
I got so hooked to it
I murmur always the thing that I cannot speak out
And pray
Looking at the Sun

Sun
Please do not come down

**It's Your Funeral**
**Howie Good**

The cemetery was located next to a busy landfill. You could stand at the graveside and see in the middle distance bulldozers crawling like insects over mountains of waste. No one remarked on the irony. She was buried forthwith in a simple pine coffin, as tradition insists. I am embarrassed that I yelled too much, but that's the sort of person I am, a roiling ultra-hot cloud of atoms. Preserve me from the people who eat the same lunch every day or who cross the street to stay away from strangers. The trip seems longer every time they make it.

## When I Try to Say I'm Sorry to Those Who Are Suffering
### Trish Lindsey Jaggers

In my head, it has a certain ring to it,
like bells in the distance, like church
getting ready to start
somewhere, a silver slice through
the clean, blue air,
no,
rather, more like a clap of thunder
against a cloudless sky
where I question whether I heard
it at all, but still, I go in, close the windows
and wait for the opening up,
for a storm to hit, hope
the wind spares the oak tree, old as Egypt,
the swing untwisting itself
on the lower branch,
the swing-path
earth worn through
to the bone of root
where I once fell,
no,
like a bird, I let go,
went singing flat through the rain
and broke my arm,
and I could hear it happen,
though I couldn't say it,
and that hurt so much
it should have bled,
it should have bled.

## Hunger
## Trish Lindsey Jaggers

Wind cools the sweat on my face
Dinner feels tight and hugged inside me
Winged things hatched once
already hungry, mouths open, eyes still shut
early life spent in a shell, fed, warmed

I know there is a word for the way rain smells
Yet is there one
for the way this air tastes
mossy, like creek rocks on the tongue?

On the path, gravel crunches, and a hunger rises
one I cannot chew away
Plantain rises up, bent from being stepped on
but alive, waiting for rain
It can't eat without it
The plantain doesn't care about rocks
Like me, it grows in the damnedest of places
the ones everything else gives up on

Petrichor. I finally thought of the word
for the smell of rain. I had to add it to Word's dictionary
so out of touch with human senses
these programs we make
thinking they'll run with or without us
as long as they don't have to eat

## Beating a Dead Horse or Waking the Dead? I Don't Know, so You Tell Me
### Trish Lindsey Jaggers

I just couldn't do it.
It took a breath, stretched
its ribs, and I could see it see me
through its lashes; life, or what mimics
life, trembled the length of its chestnut hide,
more of a quake, really, like it was wakened
trying to shake off a fly
that lit at this most inopportune time,
the way flies always fucking do,
in the middle of the night
when sleep finally arrives
on the redeye—a nod towards both
sleep-deprived eyes and early morning's joke
of a "new day," red and yellow's past argument
over tangerine's present tense,
call it a promise, one I should look forward to,
leave my night for—and then, just as the mist clears
in front of a dream I'm about to dream,
along comes a fly.
And of all the surfaces in that room,
an amalgamation of acres
of choice landing strips in the damned room,
my nose, of course, lifts,
rises to the occasion, creates a short
fly runway in the disappearing dark.
A dream never dreamt burns just outside the window
the fly gave up on.
And this fly that needs death, spoilage, to reproduce,
checks me out against the blood orange
of morning wedging through my blinds,
and chooses me to go down first.

**Sugar Skull**
**Westley Heine**

Dark avenues
like red tunnels
telescope back
into her inner eye.
Streetlights bend in
the steam of
frying bat meat.
Motel shadows
full of eyes suspend
hidden deals in
cultural force-fields.
Bugs pour from the
cracks in the mirror that
line her face with age.

She was sure she could
lead the homeless army
over the wall of the
Hollywood Forever Cemetery
to dig up the Pharaoh
and use his skull
like a radio to free
the internet slaves.
It was snowing
dope in the desert
all fangs numb
with angel feathers.
She sneezed and
blew her cover
so the cameras
descended on her
and x-rayed her soul
until she didn't believe
she ever had one.
She thought if she could
reincarnate into her enemy
and then commit suicide
she could loop time back
to before the world
was poisoned like a well.
Smoking looms of
memories flashed like
lightning in the fog
and burned her silhouette
across
the back wall of the Circle-K.
After her paranoid poems
were rejected for channeling

the dead she intoned them like
stand-up to her doctors
who decided to laugh rather
than stroke their beards, and
declared her cured, and
shaved their goats, and
bottled her tears, and
sold self-help books based on
the social media version of herself
with a close up of her
carbon footprint on the book jacket.

Pungent flowers will grow from the decay of
her good intensions, blocked orgasms,
confabulated glory days, rusted sunsets,
lying pen-pals, parent expectations,
self-inflicted lobotomies, conspiracies with
the moon, fever halos, apocalyptic codes,
bond fires with the damned,
the eulogy she wrote herself,
garbage islands, melting mushrooms,
elephants in the room, dental dams,
teddy bears, street corner prophets,
endless lists of regurgitated objectivity,
and personal madness giggling like
musical rubber numbers,
under the shade of time.
Will we ever sleep again?
Will we ever dream in a new language?
Will we ever be able to change the world but
preserve our precious melancholy mythology?
Or can peace only arrive through desolation?
Can we through trial and error,
checks and balances, be crowned with utopia
teetering on the peak of
this round of recorded history?
Torn by time, skinless, stretched
on the rack of the wheeling sun in slow mo-
tion,
teeth shattered in TV static. Shhhh, it (god)
says.

**Sleeping by the Seine**
**Westley Heine**

A sea of souls flutter just under the surface of night.
Silhouettes flicker in rolling waves like a mad carnival ride.
Whirling film of overlapping scenes are someone else's dreams.
Flying buttresses of lunging demons torpedo to oblivion.
      Who woke these webs of beards & boney branches like flayed polytheist saints?

Two thousand years of spiritual graffiti ooze in streetlights & flash-bulb skulls.
Obscene caricatures of the heart boil in Buddha-belly cauldrons.
Numb inertia of a long occupied continent gasps & gurgles.
Whispers run down the gutter thirsty for more blood & rain.
      My fractured selves crumble beneath this ancient ghost dance.

Tourists dissect symbols like meat pies and the super-ego goes cross-eyed.
Dissected center sparks fireflies, big-bang hatchlings, & lipstick on the mirror.
Where heads once rolled they drag their feet, point, grin, & photograph.
These spoiled beneficiaries of old revolutions, are wholesome vampires of time & toil,
      but still just peasants picking paper for an ever receding bottom line.

Bells & sirens hum with the rows of fleeting neon.
Cigarette butts hang in spider webs of sugar.
Woodpeckers tap Morris-code as they change the names on graves.
Making love in shadows, in mausoleums, in dioramas stacked to the sky.
      On this tectonic I can finally look over my shoulder & read left to right.

## I Forgive You For Everything I Have Done
### Eran Eads

I left somewhere
with rosemary

cooked into the belly of a fish
I am the last to finish the glass

and the rosé reminds me
not of you not of you  your eyes

pale
only fish skin left on my plate

What was it you said
this weapon's useful

How we broke the hardwood
with fucking

Your new wood contrasts
the floors. You remember me.

You shake the news
into my shoulders

in the hallway
Everyone else is damned

& everyone is a liar
& I am everyone

because I am quiet
and you want to be cruel

# First Itself Next
## Giles Goodland

**First**

First blackbird of March, tune slightly different from the year before. The first-person pronoun considers itself as old as the first organ for pushing words out, is drunk with evening's first mouthful.

The first time someone guides me there. They show me this huge white eye is the first of philosophers. The lungful of hot smoke makes my eyes first itch, obliging me to rub them; then suppurate.

Curl the hair first, then sweep it up in fill patterns. Sever the first joint of each leg: heat the face-end first to a low red heat, draw the skin off the body to the shoulders; cut the first joint off the fore-legs.

Pain first on right, then on left side of back of neck on moving head between the first position and the fibre-optic front sight. The first view one gets of Darwin is a dog playing with a ball.

Put your fists at your knees, understand them slowly and carefully for the first week or two. First, select the text, actuate the first portion of the cocking member to be moved from the first position part-way towards the second.

Fit the first computer with a mercury delay-line memory and feed rollers. Pass silently over the first moving pictures, the workers leaving the factory, flicker of a dimly captured world.

You must first find a matrix of relative loss (a matrix of grief). The first lines specify which shell to use in the long first draft which we cannot delete.

Municipal use has first priority, instream flow has third. If the overhead is considerable, record this in the first row. To do this, first activate the developer tab. Open the first pop-up menu, choose Contents, type the string.

Keats first introduces the architectural figure as a mansion of biological configuration spaces, similar to those one hears from children the first time they visit the zoo.

Racing to his first day of school, he watches gliding eagles circling a cliffside, the first to speak being the grey-eyed goddess Athēnē. The gall first appears as a small wart on the bark. The first passage quoted as poetry is actually prose.

Begin your meditations by contemplating the first card of the suit of Fire. After moving obliquely from your first firing position, direct a stream of fluid into a storage volume at a first angle, and a second stream of fluid at a second angle to induce a rotational flow of fluidized sludge.

The first day of building the chair is spent riving the green log with an axe. Winner for Best First Novel, with a 200,000-copy first printing and a seven-city tour, it describes the basic model of a robot traversing a graph which resembles the wood she traverses in the first cantos.

His first meeting with Renfield begins as the camera traces, in a long following shot, his descent to the first of two spiral gardens at Chelsea. The First Page setting refers to the first page of the document or the first page of a section.

First, the abdominal breath, and then the chest breath. The first words spring like flint shards from the axe. The somnambulist carries the sentence to his forehead, and after some effort mentions the three first letters.

The dumptrucking moon troubles the streets in first gear. The first volume consists of a collection of obituaries from a first-person perspective. It seems on first reading a bad poem, but does that mean it is actually doing something good? The seal face causes the seal liquid to be released first, indicating a seal failure.

**Itself**

The way conceals itself by being nameless
in a sentence so long it contradicts itself
if a spider lowers itself on you at night it is lucky
the bony machine thinks itself back to life
choose the symbol you want then enter the symbol itself
a wider frame to which the market itself is referable
remember the line of association controls itself
the beast stops shakes and covers itself
the sublime is within the gaze itself
the beltline hitches itself up over the rear wheel arches
a tornado screws itself on-screen, helix, vortex
the intellectual circle retracts itself day by day
divinity shows itself the more; a violent fever burns
so as to deposit itself as a thick dew, attended by
the tiny crystal spray-drop leaps of itself
the perception cannot express itself eroding
space itself is therefore sphere; a mink which
changed itself into a woman brings him food
the right hand now shows itself empty
it spreads itself out so there is scarcely any itch
the field-name may be a different length than the field itself
the elementary rapport of the brain with itself and
with fire is opposite to darkness and lights as itself
the inner of us is not the soul it is the insect head itself
a mask, the phenomenon shows itself as self-reference
the river carves a future for itself
if truth could say itself it would be said
the lamp's light wrecks itself against the inch
the wind bundles itself into a bluish cloud
the husk itself is of all-steel construction
and draws itself toward the leaf
the sentence reads itself as we listen.  The saying says
itself as one draws the body up before making a dive.
A knot straightens itself when a single tangle is undone
the moon gathers itself
raising itself on its hind legs where the dream
seals itself into backflesh slash dinosaur, see the film.

**Next**

When I revise each word into the next poem, ghosts speak to me
in the next dream I huddle inside the remarks
the next scan takes place half a turn of the wheel later, change it
to an imperative as in the next sentence
to deal with the next question, whether we need a non-monotonic logic
name it as SamplingModule and press Next. On
the next screen, create an empty lever response off the circle
and cause the spiral to reappear for the next trial.
While in this condition, see a spirit form standing next
to a gentleman leaving for the next world.
at my next sitting, after evidential statements, the medium says
you'll require a billiard ball at the next dance
and for the next half hour the room resembles a fair
so I decide to go next day and their house is full of hexagon turrets
they loosen like geese and fly honking to the next star
a dandelion carried gently towards the next weir, yelling
a pool, a vortex , the vastness between this and the next
masonry and pipes, then through the next door into a set of offices.
In the next room a woman is trapped in the stationery-cupboard.
Next time I go there on my own. It seems the owl guards
some corridor behind the ledge, a television is next to the owl.
A day or so to relax in before the next thing happens
I swipe, right to left—and IE brings up the next page.
Hold the felt-tip pen against the paper and next to the ruler.
Next day, a Thomas Hardy wind results in a total error
equivalent to the next lower accurancy class. Save
all the files, then merge them. To merge, click the next step
(Preview your merge) in Word. The next stage showcases
the core ranges of formal wear, the next disengages
the thread from the next instrument; follow it
where it goes. Into the following letter. The next.
The entrance is next to the Cave of Hearths.
Pass one chamber after the next, scramble talus fields.
Next each student is given a copy of activity sheet 3 and told
to construct the nets, and complete the next chart.
Next the trail winds uphill along an unmapped stream,
soldiers in red come next, followed by officers of the empire,
brown digester to be flung next fall on the meadow,
In the next exercise you begin to add shadows.
But the next morning his oldest boy disappears
Next time he drowns, he should carry an umbrella.
Rebirth is the name of the next breath.

**\*\***
**Tali Cohen Shabtai**

The scent of hollow pipe
Waves slowly through the crowded space of my
Room.

And the embroidered candlestick placed
In its domain
Smooths over the chill-
The emptiness

And everything is so
Stifled
So
Personal
So chained one
To another.

## My Permanent Record
## Jim Tritten

I was in a long queue, waiting my turn in line. In my left hand was an *Aviators Flight Log Book* (OPNAV Form 3760-31 Rev 4-65). I opened it to the aircraft mishap section in the back and looked down.

| | |
|---|---|
| **Date** 7 Mar 69 | **Model of aircraft** EA-1F |
| **Damage** E | **Primary cause factor** Pilot/Fatigue |
| **Remarks** Flap idler link failed. Combination of overstress and previous fatigue of part due to overstress | |
| **Entry approved** R.L. Lofton, Commanding | |

It documented an error on my part – one forever available for any logs and records yeoman, operations officer, or commanding officer to read. I made a mistake when flying and had lowered the flaps on my airplane at too high an airspeed. Doing so broke a piece of one of the linkages that made the flaps work.

I shuffled forward as the line moved.

We all make mistakes. How many of us were told in high school if we kept doing something, or not doing something, those things would become a part of our permanent record? I did my share of time in Principal Cavanaugh's office. *My God, did they send my permanent record to every new company when I applied for a job?*

If I make a criminal mistake with the law, the desk sergeant will dutifully record the transgression in a book. That's what they say, right? "Book 'em, Danno." If found guilty, or not, some court stenographer will use a chorded keyboard to record the decision. Eventually, the record will be transcribed for others to read. Unless you are a juvenile and your file is confidential. Or you enter the Witness Protection Program and are sent to live in Rio Rancho, New Mexico.

When my father was in the U.S. Navy, he had a personnel record. Twenty years after his death, I wrote to the National Personnel Records Center and paid a few dollars. They sent me his file. I learned a lot about my father from reading what various officers and chief petty officers said about his service. I wonder if he ever cleared his record with his bookie before he passed on.

Do we all have multiple records, or does someone maintain a single master permanent record where all these things are compiled? Is there a way to expunge entries with which we disagree? I'm sure everyone has work evaluations they would like to go away. Or an entry in a U.S. Navy pilot's log book recording how he had lowered the flaps while the airspeed was too fast and broke an idler link.

Is my *aw shit I broke the flaps* balanced out by multiple personal awards, citations, letters of commendation, promotions, and the like? Just how many *atta boys* cancel out one small aw shit? How many if the transgression is really egregious? Can we convert to Catholicism right before the end, confess, and say a few Hail Marys as penance? How about making a sizeable donation to the charity of the Pope's choice? No wait, I'm Presbyterian, and I think I remember reading something about predestination at Sunday School many years ago.

The line moved and I shuffled forward some more. Only a few more until it'd be my turn.

If you go for a job, it is likely someone will gain access to some part of your records. Certainly, the federal government checks whether a degree was in fact earned, or whether your experience listed on the job application is as truthful as you described. I remember at least one individual who lied about having a doctorate on her job application and got away with it. At the time, she proudly told friends she had listed an earned Ph.D. on her application to beat out some disabled veteran on the civil service ranking system. Did both her job and lying to get it make it into her permanent record?

There were still two folks in front of me on line. I opened another of my navy pilot's log book to see if someone had recorded an aircraft crash on the mishap page. An accident far more severe than causing a flap idler link to fail. Interestingly, the record of mishaps in that log book is blank. Lax logs and records yeoman? Commanding officer trying to give me a break? Years later, I obtained a redacted copy of the accident report from the Naval Safety Center. They had a record of what happened despite the mishap never making it into my pilot's log book. Everyone in the squadron knew, even if it wasn't in my log book. If other people were aware of what had happened to me, was it cross-filed into my permanent record?

Maybe there isn't some master fusion complex where all the things we have done – some of which we would like to forget – are totaled up. Plusses and minuses. Naughty and nice. A comprehensive list of all that was good and bad. Perhaps recording all these entries into a single file with everything there is to know about a person is just too complicated for the average mortal and his databases. Problem is, I know.

When I was finally at the head of the line, I saw an elderly man stooped over a desk, a nameplate engraved in gold before him. He had waist-length white hair, a long beard, and a drooping mustache. He wore a white robe. I hung my head; my hands clasped in front of me around my log books, and as contrite an expression on my face as I could manage. He called my name and lifted a single bushy white eyebrow. I raised my head and looked into his penetrating cobalt blue eyes. He opened a voluminous tome that thudded as it fell open on the desk. Dust rose in the air; he blew away a small cloud. He coughed and waved his hands to clear the air. "Let's see what we have here." St. Peter tilted up the hardcover black book. I saw the title – *Permanent Record of James John Tritten*.

# THE BIRTHDAY GIFTS
## Debbie De Louise

Jeannie and Jenny were as different as identical twins could be. Fifty years ago, their mother went into labor during a Halloween party. Their father, dressed as Mickey Mouse, dashed his Minnie to the hospital where she gave birth to always prompt Jeannie at 11:45 p.m. on October 31 and never-on-time Jenny at Midnight.

As Jeannie and Jenny grew, their parents noticed the differences in their two daughters and nurtured their individualities. Jenny was good with words, speaking earlier than Dr. Spock recommended and chattering with an advanced vocabulary from that point on. Jeannie, on the other hand, was astute with numbers. Although a late reader, she could count and calculate mathematical concepts from a very young age. Her favorite activity was cooking with her mother where she would measure ingredients and allocate precise servings to the four members of her family.

It was no wonder that Jenny became a librarian. With her nose in books most of the time, the library profession attracted her like a magnet to metal. Her parents were so happy with her decision that they readily paid for her to attend college and library school. They were proud when she landed the job of reference librarian at their local public library.

Jeannie's career path took a different turn. She wanted to be a chemist, but despite studying hard for her entrance exams, she was not a good test taker like Jenny. Her second choice was culinary school, and, when she was accepted, her parents agreed to pay for her tuition, as well. After all, they didn't want to play favorites, although everyone knew that Jenny was daddy's girl and Jeannie was mom's.

As far as dating and marriage, neither girl was lucky initially. Jenny, who wore glasses and dressed in long skirts with her hair tied in a librarian's bun, didn't attract many suitors. She finally met a library patron named Stanley who was studying computer science. While Jenny was verbally profuse, Stanley was a quiet man. However, opposites sometimes attract, and the two of them married at 30 years old.

A year after Jenny tied the knot, Jeannie, who dressed in popular fashion with her long hair loose, met a fellow cook named Antoine who brought her to France to meet his family. Not much of a conversationalist, Jeannie could think of nothing to discuss with Antoine's parents except cooking and baking. His mother, a French model, found that talk rather boring. She had higher hopes for her son imagining he would follow in the footsteps of his artist father and marry a French woman. But Jeannie and Antoine were in love and married shortly later under the Eiffel Tower with a small reception at a French restaurant. Jeannie's parents and sister, who were afraid of airplanes, did not attend.

Since Jenny shared her parents' fear of flying, the two sisters didn't see one another often except when Jeannie was able to close the restaurant that she and Antoine opened in Paris so she could visit her family back in New York. It was, however the sisters' custom to send one another a gift on their birthdays. Jeannie made sure that the package for Jenny would arrive on October 31 each year. Jeannie's gift from Jenny often arrived a week later, not due to mail delivery issues in France, but because Jenny always mailed it late.

Jenny and Jeannie had no children. Jenny's husband, Stanley, who became a millionaire from some stocks he purchased from Microsoft in the 1980's and the assets from his own computer firm, died in a car accident driving to a computer conference in Manhattan. Jenny inherited it all plus the benefits from Stanley's life insurance policy and bought an estate on the North Shore of Long Island where she kept several cats and a library of books.

Jeannie and Antoine's restaurant didn't attract enough diners and closed its doors a month before Jeannie's 50th birthday. Antoine's parents refused to lend him any financial support to open another business, and Antoine, in despair, shot himself in their tiny apartment when Jeannie was at the grocer's.

Jeannie didn't want to go back to the States because she had become so used to her life in France. Not as adept at languages as her sister, she had had a hard time communicating at first, but most of the French people she met spoke English. After Antoine's death, she had very little money but wanted to open a bakery which she believed would do better than their restaurant. She asked Jenny for a loan, but her sister, who relied on an accountant to handle her money, refused to finance the endeavor considering it foolish. Instead, she appealed to Jeannie to come back to New York and live with her, but Jeannie was allergic to cats and was happy in her small apartment where memories of Antoine were still fresh.

Since both their parents were gone now, Jeannie had no one else to ask for help. She felt her sister was being selfish and recalled how Jenny had always confiscated her dolls and toys when they were young. Jeannie had always been the one who shared more easily - dividing their allowances into two separate piles – cutting their mother's pies into two equal slices – separating their chores into similarly manageable tasks.

Now, as Jeannie picked up the bottle of pills her doctor had recommended for the depression she was experiencing after Antoine's death, she contemplated what to send Jenny for her 50th birthday the following week. At home, she decided to bake two small birthday cakes. One for her sister and one for herself. She measured each ingredient precisely and ground up all the pills from her prescription along with some rat poison she had in the apartment to deal with the rodents because she and Antoine couldn't have cats because of her allergies. She added equal spoonfuls into the mix. What a true surprise it would be for her greedy sister. For once, she thought Jenny would be at a loss for words when she ate Jeannie's specially prepared birthday present. When she knew Jenny had received her birthday gift, Jeannie would bake the second cake for herself from the frozen batter she'd saved, eat a slice, and join Antoine in the small French cemetery where he was buried.

Calculating the French mail delivery, as she had for many years previously, Jeannie expected Jenny's package to arrive on October 31. On that day, she baked the second cake. As she ate it, the mail arrived with a letter from overseas. It had her sister's address on it. Jenny often wrote Jeannie letters, pages of them filled with her chatty banter that Jeannie had little time or desire to answer. In fact, she'd stopped reading them altogether in the last few months. She decided to open this one, however, because she knew it would be the final stupid letter from Jenny. It was dated on the day Jeannie had mailed Jenny the birthday package. This one was shorter than Jenny's usual letters. It read:

Dear Jeannie,

I know our birthdays are coming soon, but, this year, instead of sending you a gift, I have decided to visit you in person. I have conquered my fear of flying by seeing a hypnotherapist. I have also found loving homes for all my cats and sold my estate on Long Island. My accountant has procured a chateau not far from Paris where I would like to invite you to live with me. I have reconsidered your request and have put aside money for you to open a bakery if you still wish to do so. After all, you only live once, and what are sisters for?

*Happy birthday, my dearest sister.*

*p.s. I wanted this to be a surprise but, because I wasn't able to get a flight to make it in time for our birthdays, I'm sending this letter ahead of my departure on November 1st. For once, I am hoping it arrives in time for your birthday. I was going to call you, but I had my phone disconnected after the house sale. I still haven't gotten around to purchasing a cell phone because you know how I hate devices with numbers. So I guess this will be our last communication until we are together once again.*

*Jenny*

Jeannie stared at the words in her sister's letter as she tasted the birthday cake on her tongue. Figuring how long it would take to digest the ingredients, Jeannie calculated she would be dead by midnight.

THE END

## Maui in a Moment
## Audrey Rauth

Sunlight streamed through the soft clouds, speckling the sprawling field of grass with patches of light amongst shadow. We ran barefoot along the red dirt path, winding between tree branches and groupings of lava rock. The breeze reached down to stroke our faces lightly and twisted our hair as it lifted back up. Quickly we came to the edge of the bluff. It overlooked the ocean of gradient blues divided by bubbling lines of white waves rushing towards the black sand beach below. To our right was a natural pool, separated from the ocean by a thin band of grey lava rock which was slowly shrinking as the tide grew higher. In the middle of the pool stood a single rock island with what looked to be steps made of stone spiraling up the sides. "This is heaven," I thought. There was nothing more beautiful that I had ever seen.

My younger sister turned quickly and smiled at me, sun lit her face. She took off running toward the twisted red dirt path that led to the natural pool, flitting back and forth through the waving grasses along her way. I followed. With sure footing, we let the path lead us closer to the glistening water below. After navigating through low-hanging branches and over-grown roots, the path failed to lead us any farther. as if urging us to jump, the red dirt pointed straight over the edge of the rock into the aqua water below. We looked at each other and, without words, knew exactly what would come next.

Not bothering to prepare myself for the fall, I pushed my body away from land, into air. It happened in slow motion. The sun in my eyes and my face full of wind. My hair twisted into knots and I was floating. I felt the cool water surround my skin, soothing and fresh. It swallowed me and for a moment I felt nothing. I kicked my legs and resurfaced, greeted by laughter from my sister and Mother Nature's wispy touch of wind across my cheeks.

Reaching through the water, silky and clear, we swam toward the lone rock island in the middle of the pool. Once there, my feet brushed against smooth stone and the water fell away from my skin as I stood up. Steps of lava rock ascended the island, wrapping tightly around the outside edge as if for support. We walked slowly, stepping carefully along the way. The rock was rough against my feet and warm to the touch. We followed the spiral staircase a few steps more.

Almost as if it were taken straight from a child's drawing, there was a single palm tree atop the island surrounded by grains of smooth black sand, shimmering. The palm tree had lush green leaves with long finger-like fronds, dancing in the sky and reaching toward the sun. My sister and I sat in the sand, facing the sprawling ocean and smiled, completely at peace with the moment.

# Haunted
## Maddie Anderlik

perhaps i'm being haunted. the other night my sister and i both heard a noise at the same time. at first, it sounded like someone was walking on the stairs, but usually you can hear them go all the way down or all the way up. each step has its own unique cheap suburban creak. but i only heard a few creaks, like someone took a few steps and stopped. a little while later i thought i heard someone going into the bathroom. but usually you can hear the door click shut, you can hear the wood scraping against the purple rug as it opens and closes. all i could hear was the knob moving, like someone put a hand on it but decided not to use it.

my sister thought someone was breaking in. i went downstairs but there was no one there, all the doors were still locked. i even checked my mom's bedroom to make sure no one was in there. the next morning my aunt told me she had gone downstairs to let the dog out, but she hadn't used the bathroom. so why did the knob turn?

last night i dreamt about a ghost. i don't remember it all, but i remember i talked to her in my refrigerator. i opened the door and i could hear her inside. she was murdered, and she told me how she died. the truth was in the clay, a bit of clay and sand in a plastic bag tacked to a bulletin board. i ran downstairs to tell everyone about the ghost. i knew that if i was right about the clay, then that proved i had talked to her- that i had the truth. right as i was opening the bag, i woke up. and i knew i was waking up as it happened. it was almost as if i had a choice- that there was this moment where i was in dream limbo, stuck between consciousness and sleep. my eyes were closed and i was still in my dream, but i was aware that it was a dream, and i could open my eyes and break out, or i could try to push deeper into my sleep in search of the truth. i woke up.

perhaps i'm being haunted. i'm crying more than usual. i've thought of my father more in the past few days than i have my entire life, or at least that's what it feels like. i don't know why. this time has no significance to him, not that i know of anyway.

i always write at three am. sometimes when i get the urge to write in the middle of the night i look at the clock and it always seems to be three am. i don't know what that means. lately i find myself awake at three am almost every night and sometimes it's the happiest time of the day because its not weird that i'm home in my room doing nothing and everyone is asleep and the house is quiet. i once heard someone say that the veil between this world and the next is thinnest at three am. i think about that a lot.

## After a Century of Pushups
### Thomas M. McDade

"Rabbit's Foot won't run off with me the way Honest Harry did the other day, Bobby," said Katie. I'd written "Tom" repeatedly on her back as if my fingertip were a dull pencil, told her my name several times. "I'll rate him a perfect quarter tomorrow. Thanks for the massage." She'd requested one after doing 100 pushups and collapsing. We stayed in position. I traced her forehead, sharp nose, hesitated on her cheekbones, taut earlobes and harp neck top of her ear that was flush against her head. As I touched her chin, she ground her teeth. She tugged up a smile. Her breath went sleepy. I stood, took a pink crib sized blanket off the bed and covered her legs. I kissed my fingers and touched her cheek: lovely. I hesitated before leaving, hoping she'd flip over, and laughing say, "Had you fooled didn't I, Tom?" and so on. I slipped off as quietly as any escapee from an asylum or thief from a crime scene. I was spacey, almost drove away without caulking a small third floor window. Just as I put the tip of the gun into the gap, a mob of wasps shot out. One forehead sting was all but trying to slap them away almost sent me to my grave.

I tried to untwist all that had gone on with Katie that morning as I drove to the track but couldn't find its beginning, middle or end. I was too late to check out the horses in the paddock. I bet according to her sure thing info. Each of the fifty dollar bills she'd given me had "Love you Bobby" written in red ink. When would I be "Tom" again? The horses were entering the track. It came to me that Jeep Hurry was a classic quitter, often led deep into the stretch, then backed up. J. K. Marcher, who had a bad reputation but still managed work, was up on the 11-year-old. He must have a fast talking agent. Marcher had served suspensions for "Failing to give his best effort," and "Reporting to jockey quarters in a condition unfit to accept his mounts." He peeked at the odds as he passed the tote: 60-1. The race was over a distance of ground, a mile and seventy yards. The gate crew had a tough time loading Burnt Hills. Jeep Hurry eased in as if it were his stable stall. The field broke well except for Our Rocker who stumbled but recovered. More Music showed the early foot, took a 3-length advantage at the clubhouse turn. The rest bunched up except for Jeep Hurry who ambled along behind Gunwale a half-length, but soon Marcher with one crack of the whip had his charge gaining prosperously. York Road joined More Music and they matched each other stride for stride, Greek Lover a distant third. At the top of the stretch, I envisioned Katie as the rider. Jeep Hurry passed tiring rivals and continued to advance. He collared the leaders at the eighth pole. York Road faltered badly. In a sudden lurch, Jeep Hurry dispatched More Music and breezed across the finish line 4 1/2 lengths to the good. Marcher rode him out to the clubhouse turn. I figured he had a buzzer to ditch. Booing drowned out the few wild cheers from the crowd. York Road was a 3-5. When his jockey dismounted, a drunk threw a beer can that narrowly missed. I would have been excited had I picked the horse myself, unaware of the outcome but thanks Katie anyway. Each ticket was worth $122, I opened an account at the Blackstone Valley Credit Union.

Four days passed before more Carpenter Street work. Jimmy, my boss, was waiting with Dunkin Donuts coffees. A second floor apartment just vacated needed an abracadabra paint job. Yes, Katie's, some men would have jumped up to click heels as many times as possible, off the hook, decent helping of do-re-mi. What in hell was wrong with me? We climbed the stairs. Jimmy marked off what to paint with a piece of chalk. "Don't bother with the ceiling," he said. "You could eat off of it. Skip the latrine it's a showpiece. Selective is the magic word."

Jimmy doctored K-Mart off-white to the consistency of milk. Shortly you could call me homogenized. It was like painting over the fright in a haunted house. My brain was a cornfield maze. Done at noon, I couldn't wait to get myself to Rock's Bar to tie one on. I made my last trip to the bathroom. The hot water was tepid. I shook my hands dry. Katie's hairbrush on the floor startled me like a roach that big would.

Two more weeks to master house painting to Jimmy's satisfaction. He made me a specialist, window sashes. Yes, I was always hoping to spot Katie through a pane. I drove by Lincoln Downs when I figured morning workouts were over for the wish of her. It was at Kip's Diner one morning that a clue popped. I overheard a cop telling a short order cook that he'd cashed a big bet on a horse named Diana V at the Marshfield Fair, ridden by a girl jock, a former exercise rider at Lincoln Downs, named White, couldn't recall her first. She'd never told me her last name.

Saturday, I had a late breakfast in my car, bran muffins and coffee from the Stop & Shop. I filled up at Costa's Sunoco. I got on I-95 at the Newport Ave entrance, sixty-miles to Marshfield. I expected mobbed stands since it was the final day of racing, cloudy but mild, not so. I rented binoculars, bought a *Racing Form* and a program. No rider named White. I wagered distractedly but with some success, hit the Double for forty-nine dollars, French Apple and Con Gusto. At the Beer Garden, I overheard a tall old fellow wearing a Red Sox cap telling his wife about Katie White splitting for Midwest tracks under contract to the trainer J. J. Holly. "I guess those four wins on Diana V went to both their heads," said the woman. I was happy Katie had finally gotten her jockey's license.

"Good for her to slip out of these parts. Imagine life after your brother murders your parents, sets the house to blazes. To think Bobby used to work on my car at Thorpe's Garage."

"You'll be interrupting your Last Rites with that highlight," snapped his mate.

I choked on a swallow of beer. "You all right son," asked the Sox fan? I was stunned and for all the wrong reasons. I was used, a pinch hitter, a stunt man for a killer. Ha! I can break the law as I please. He'll do my time. What a sap. Were there other surrogates? Then, I pictured her doing her pushups, wanting my touch. She gave me money and the hot tip. "Calm down, selfish son-of-a-bitch" I muttered to myself. Christ, she lost her parents. How would I have handled a like tragedy? Self-righteous bastard, a one-morning stand your goal. I wandered around in a fog. The track could have been a merry-go-round. I split as the horses were loading for the sixth race, gave my Daily Double money to the nun shaking change in a Maxwell House coffee can.

I blasted Top-40; welcomed that invasion to crowd my mind. I hit a pothole and the station jumped to gospel music. I prayed for Katie and I saw a light but it took a week or so until it shined bright enough. For a split second, I was her brother Bobby; the fifty bucks and hot tip meant for a fantasy getaway. Was *she* in on the murders? I got away all right, used the money for a Caribbean cruise. I splurged on several massages. A couple of times the poundings of masseuse hands sounded like far off hoofbeats and I felt like dirt.

# BECOMING A LIFEGUARD
## Marlene Tully

It wasn't one of those jobs that I went looking for. It was just something that I kind of fell into. Not too long ago, I got kicked out of the pool of life. Everyone was splashing around having a good time and I could no longer swim in the deep end, much less let go of the edge of the pool. I heard a whistle blow and someone yelled, "Outta the pool!" and I left. I've been sitting on the edge of the pool watching everyone ever since. I am feeling quite envious of their lives. My own life seems so limited and useless. It's been two years since the whistle blew for me to get out of the pool. I tried to go back once. I pretended to be swimming, but in fact, I nearly drowned again.

I look back over the water and for the first time I can see that some of the swimmers in the pool are flailing about. Do they know they are in trouble? I can see it. It is all crystal clear to me. They are unaware of the dangers that lurk beneath the waters, the same dangers that altered my life forever. I know exactly what they are doing, because I have been there myself.

"Hey!" I want to yell to them, "Outta the pool!"

I'm not a lifeguard. I'm supposed to be worried about saving myself, not to be concerned with others. Hell, I don't even know if I can swim anymore.

"Hey!" I can't contain myself any longer, "Listen to me!"

The sound of my voice is lost over the loud splashing of the waves throughout the pool. I look around. There is no lifeguard on duty. There's only an empty chair and thousands of people in the pool. Way too many people are in the deep end. I see others around the perimeter of the pool, many are self absorbed on their phones, putting on suntan lotion, a few are immersed in conversation and drinking, completely unaware that there are men and women about to drown. I run up to the man taking a selfie, "Please! You have to rescue them. If you let them be they will drown. We will lose them!"

He scowls at me and moves to better light for his picture. I go up the a couple applying suntan lotion to each other, "Excuse me!" I so desperately want their attention. They move their chairs, as if they don't even see me. Or perhaps they didn't want to see me.

I begin to yell at the top of my lungs, "Who will rescue the rescuers?!"

I am quite the spectacle. I can feel all eyes are on me, but no one says a word. I divert my attention back to the ailing swimmers. I take a deep breath. I walk over to the gate in the fence. Everyone is expecting me to leave. I have failed. I no longer have the courage to dive into the deep end. They know it. They turn back to their phones, their lotions, and their drinks knowing it was only a matter of time before I left. But I don't' leave. There is a life saving ring with a rope tied to it next to the gate. I grab hold of the rope and realize I cannot leave my kindred spirit floundering in the water alone. I have become the lifeguard. With all of my strength, I hurl the ring out into the pool, tightly holding onto the rope. The swimmer stares at me and feels the connection. He knows I will not let him drown. I drag him in and he holds onto the rim of the pool, feeling safer than he has in a long time. I hold out my hand and his grip tightens around mine as I pull his exhausted body from the water.

"Thanks," he mutters as he falls onto the hot cement slab, trying to catch his breath.

A few minutes pass and he asks, "Why did you save me? You don't even know me. "

"I do know you," I said. "I swam in the deep end once too, you know. I've walked in your shoes and I swore no one else would ever swim in the pool without a lifeguard."

"You saved my life. How can I repay you?" He asks feeling as if he owes me.

"I put up my hands, "No, I didn't save your life. That is something only you can do for yourself. I just helped give you a chance by offering a friendly hand. I couldn't leave you all alone out there in the water. It just didn't seem fair."

"You must be an excellent swimmer!" He said in awe.

"I was at one time. Now I no longer swim."

He stared incredulously at me; unable to comprehend that the person who helped him doesn't even swim.

"Do you miss the water?" He asked.

"At first I did. I was jealous that everyone else seemed to be having a great time without me. Then I realized there were far too many people who were ready to drown and there was no lifeguard to save them. I am still an integral part of the pool, the part that everyone takes for granted and ignores. I see danger when no one lese perceives it. I sense when someone is in real trouble. I may never be able to swim carefree again, but I am doing something much more important now."

"What's that?"

I used to wonder, 'Who would rescuers the rescuers?' I now know the answer, I will."

"That's a lot of work for one person."

"I'm not alone. Very soon, you will be a lifeguard too. Unfortunately, there are many more that need to be rescued, but once they are, they will help keep the pool safe. We'll use they buddy system. Now rest, I'll save your spot. You'll be back and you'll be a much stronger swimmer then you have ever been."

The man smiled at me and turned to walk away. He turned back, making sure I wasn't a figment of his imagination. I looked at him directly in they eyes and he was reassured he would have company along his arduous journey to recovery. He picked up a town and started to wipe himself down, eager to find his way back to the pool and to his new noble profession of being a lifeguard.

# Head Hunted
## June Hunter

I should have known when I saw the hunting 'literature' on the occasional table in the reception area. It was more than a clear indication of the type of person I would be working for. Not at all the type of waiting area publications I would have expected to see in an Accountant's practice. It was the promise of the 'Managerial position' though, with my own office that drew me to the job. Not to mention the hefty salary increase and the proposed training programme that would help to enhance my career.

*"We would very much value your expertise,"* is what he had said over the phone. *"We're confident that you'll fit in well with the rest of the staff."* No face-to-face interview was required. *"We've done our research, and we know you'll be perfect for the job."* I was surprised but flattered and, without too much consideration or hesitation, I resigned from the stale, stagnant, under-valued, under-paid position I had held for five years.

So I didn't browse through any of the glossy *Hunting* or *Shooting Gazette* periodicals while I waited in the reception area on my first day. Totally ignored the magnificent buck on the front cover of one of them, antlers standing proud. Had no interest in learning how to mimic the grunts of a mature buck. Instead I kept my eyes firmly on the painting on the wall opposite me: A deer silhouetted against a backdrop of the setting sun. Or, it could have been the rising sun. I had no way of knowing. I kept my thoughts focussed on the name tag that would soon appear on my own office door, with the word 'Manager' right underneath.

I had been waiting for about ten minutes when a woman came tottering down the passage on heels so high that she could easily have been walking on stilts. "Sorry to keep you waiting," she said. "I'm Moira." As she reached out to shake my hand she toppled off one of her heels and lurched, lopsided, right into me. I grabbed her elbow before she could topple any further. "Sorry," she said, as she searched the carpet for the culprit. "Damn paper clips." Then turned back to me with a smile so full of whiteness I was almost blinded. "Chuck's ready to see you now."

I followed her as she escorted me down the passage, past several open office doors where the occupants were bent over papers on their desks, or peering at their computer screens while tapping away on the keyboard. No one looked up as I passed.

It was at the point when I walked into Chuck's office that I really should have turned around and walked out again. It wasn't the mess of papers and files on every surface, and in every corner, and under every piece of furniture. I'd heard that a messy office indicates a genius is at work. It wasn't even the stale tobacco smell that seemed to thicken the air in the room, despite the window being wide open. Or the matter of fact way Chuck tipped the files off a chair onto the floor so that I could sit down. None of these things phased me at all. No. It was the massive stag trophy on the wall above his head that looked as if it had only that morning pushed itself through the wall with its pointy antlers, and got stuck at the shoulders.

"Glad to have you on board," said Chuck with an outstretched, nicotine-stained hand. I said nothing as I slumped into the seat he had cleared, and watched the door close behind Moira's retreating heels.

"You do seem to have a good deal of experience," he said, as he fidgeted with the corner of the single page in front of him. "According to your LinkedIn profile you've worked in Accountancy for a number of years."

"I do have a more comprehensive CV here," I said, offering him my six page resume.

"Not necessary," he said. "I saw all the career info I needed to see when I head-hunted you."

The large, glassy eyes of the stag on the wall above him seemed to simper with a wise, all-knowing gaze.

"I know what your strong points are. So tell me. What sort of things really get your back up? What it is that you can definitely not abide, under any circumstances?"

I glanced at the dead animal above him, and wondered why he would ask such a question. I guessed it was because he needed to get to know me better as an individual; or perhaps he was expecting me to react to his hobby. "Well I'll be honest with you," I said. "I can't stand sniffing. For some reason the sound just sends my nerves sparking."

He twitched his nose from side to side and scratched his top lip.

"Oh, and bored, mobile phone addicted teenagers who can't take responsibility for their own faults. Especially those who speak in that groany voice, as if they've just been woken up from a very deep sleep."

His bottom lip trembled. "Sniffers?" He said.

"Yes. Persistent sniffers. Those who won't use a handkerchief. I really can't abide that sort of person." "Right," he said, pushing himself up from his chair. "Let me show you where everything is, and who you'll be working with."

As I followed him from room to room I wondered why he introduced me as 'our newest member of staff' instead of 'our new Manager'. I noticed, too, that there were no empty offices at all.

"We've done a bit of a reshuffle," he said, as we approached the last office. "This will be your spot, right here." He gestured towards a desk in the corner. "And these are your minions." At a long table on the other side of the room sat six recruits who barely looked up from their mobile phones. "They've recently joined us as interns, and are full of enthusiasm to learn all they can from you."

As I looked from him to them and back again, I was sure I could see a little twitch of a smile at the corner of his mouth.

"You want me to train them?" I said.

"That's right. Now, I'll leave you to get settled in. If you have any questions talk to Jackie, in the next office. She's the Practice Manager. She'll sort you out."

"But you said I..." Too late. He was gone.

When I turned back the minions were all watching me. Their hostile eyes beaming from spotty, vapid faces. I folded my arms and stared at them. "Have you had any accounting experience at all?"

"No," they all groaned at once.

"It's not our fault, though," said one, and they all groaned in agreement.

Then one of them sniffed. One of those slippery, slithery, snorts that always made me feel the urge to swallow.

I didn't need an escort to find my way back along the passage to the reception area. Moira was at her desk talking into the phone, one stiletto heeled foot crossed over the other. She looked up with a frown, as I waved and left the building.

## The Dating Etiquette of Snails
### Ben Mcnair

'He used to turn me on, but now he just turns my stomach'.

I hear her, she has been speaking like this for more than 15 minutes. There have been another three calls that my colleagues have taken. All sound so much better than mine. It is a Wednesday night, 8.30pm. It is not a busy time for desperate people, like a Friday night, or a Sunday evening would be. That is when people say they need the most help. At Samaritans we are the friendly voice that listens. We listen, we don't judge, we don't hector. The voice people turn to when they feel desperate, or lonely. Not usually suicidal, but at times when they need a sympathetic voice, or someone to tell them where to turn to next.

I know the voice, that is the worst of it. She and her husband live down the road. They are the Street's soap opera. Always shouting and slamming doors. It has been like this for years, but she has only been phoning on a Wednesday night for the past three months. Obviously, she does not know it is me. We don't have anything in common, except for the Snails that live in the gardens, and never seem to go, in spite of the traps that are put out for them. I know more than is necessary, but she seems to need an outlet for her complaints, as he does not listen, is not the man she married, is too busy with work to notice their home. She even tells me about the affair she was contemplating, but then says she loves him too much to do anything about it.

If anyone else had accepted her call, I would have been none the wiser, but that is the way of these things. A million things line up to one certainty.

I wish I did not know this. There are a couple of other people who I am expecting calls from tonight, and if they don't phone you don't know what is happening. Either they could have out-grown you, found some sort of perspective, or taken the difficult way out. We touch so many lives in these four walls, the six of us, but it is like Jury duty. We cannot speak about it, to anyone. So, people unload their little bag of troubles on us, and then we have a little more to carry with us every day.

We just have to hope that are doing some good here.

She hangs up suddenly, does not even say goodbye. The line just goes dead. She is always doing that, so I think nothing more of it.

One of the calls I was expecting comes through. He had just been made redundant, but now had a new job, and a girl he met is going with him to the cinema. He thanks me for listening, and invites me out for a pint. I politely decline, we have to keep our anonymity here. The other call I was expecting does not come. I hope it is a good sign, but I suspect it might not be, and we will never know either way. We just have to hope we are doing some good here.

I am meant to finish at 10.00pm, but I wait around a bit longer. The phones are not busy, and in the current climate, we have to expect them to be. It is a sign of the times that we get busy when Society goes to the wall. We don't even have leaders who can help these days.

I get home just past 11.00pm that night. The street is cordoned of, and I see police cars, and an ambulance. The Husband is there, and I see he is covered in blood. I think it is her blood, but I can't be sure. He sees me, and the neighbours. He is subdued, and shaking. He is covered in a blanket, as the ambulance men wheel her out on their trolley. She is awake, but seems weakened.

The Police man tells me she had attempted Suicide, but how her husband had stopped her, and called the Ambulance. He says that they believe his story, but they will still be carrying out an investigation, just to make sure she isn't in any real trouble with him.

The Police Man said they had been having problems. He said someone else was involved. Someone she spoke to, said he was helping her through it.

We just have to hope that are doing some good here.

## My Mud Season
## Lisa Rosenblatt

Mountain peaks rise, shaping the horizon, wind catches the branches and needles of the pines at the edge of the yard. The slender stems hanging over the fence vibrate, sway, dance in the breeze. Her radio on the table plays a steady mix of light pop and deathly, grisly electronic rock. She's pulled out her computer, is trying to figure out how to insert a picture to renew her passport. There used to be someone to do things like this, there were servants and admirers, but for a long time now she's had to do things like this for herself. Or at least try.

"You need a cord, a connecting cord—for the new renewal application, you need a cord," I say and try to avoid using the word dongle because I know that will throw her. Even without my mentioning dongle, she gives up, closes the computer, and picks up the phone. It's an old landline phone. Pretty soon it's going to be an antique and maybe it will be worth something, because she's never moved on to cell phones and smart phones and that phone is going on fifty now. Other than a few chips and a crack from when she threw it, the phone is fine, and its ring is genuinely like a phone ring, like the ring tone that people put on their cell phones when they want it to sound like the old ringing of a telephone. When she answers, she puts on a fake voice to ward off the robocalls, or the police, or the tax office, or whoever might be out to get her, although everyone can tell it is her, as not many people living high up in the Alps have a woman's fake deep voice with a posh British accent.

She tells me later, after she puts down the phone, "Max says he is running around like a chicken with his head cut off." I assume he's had to fly again from London to Munich or Paris or Frankfurt and he probably forgot his luggage again or forgot to get on the plane for the next leg of his journey. He knows her number by heart. We will hear it in great detail next week when he returns and sits inside, smoking a joint with her, a huge fat one that she really can't handle but that's why he comes over, to have someone to smoke a huge fat joint with as he tells the story waving his arms, waiting for her to laugh at all the excruciatingly snobbish parts. His hair is thinning.

The dog farts. "It's not about winning," I suddenly say out loud, although I have absolutely no idea what it *is* about.

Snow is still clinging on, capping the peaks of the Alps, running down the sides, creating veins to pump the water into the valleys. Patches of earth have dried and gathered the heat of the sun, others are still saturated from the melting snow. The earth slushing, slogging in the excess, sudden flowing, you can catch the pungent damp odor of spring if you walk into the woods. It's muddy and messy and does not look at all like the advertising brochures or the photos inside the oversized photo books on the coffee table in the main house, but maybe a touch like the cover photo that's torn at the edges, water stains on the Alps, yellow tinge to the white of the clouds.

There is probably a name for this. When she starts to get restless and tries to renew her passport. When I come to visit to smell the spring. I'm here now, I come here quite often, so I probably should know it, the name for it. Here, in this place where I left a part of me so many years ago, a part that I can no longer pick up and take with me anymore because it is now more a part of the place than of me. I was a tourist here and I worked here and I lived here or so I thought, but never really cut off my feet and dug the stumps of my legs into the soil and let the blood flowing from the open flesh join with the blood flowing up from the earth and grow roots as they say, be-come of the soil. I never did that. My being always remained on the surface, to be easily brushed away. But she, she would have cut her feet off and melded with the soil of the place, would have grown the roots if she'd known that that' how it's done. After all, she's planted herself firmly here. She refuses to wear the apron, the whole having chickens running around, all of that, but she is most definitely here. Even being the crackpot crazed witch in the hills would be better than what she is now.

It is too late, though, because she never cut her feet off as no one ever told her that that is how you do it, and although she thinks she knows all the secrets there are, as she is a hexe, with magical potions and spells that she spits out between yellowed teeth, gnarled fingers holding red feathers gesticulating wildly over a threadbare upholstered throne, she never caught on to the blood and the soil as something that she could actually do, and even though her great grandfather was, or shook hands with, the Red Baron she once whispered as an aside, and someone along the way bought a royal crest, what does that have to do with blood and soil and why would she want to grow peasant roots? Except for the fact that she wants to, wants to like an old farmer woman wants to milk the cows and chop wood, it makes no sense. Like the dongle to her. Her want becomes a flower patch of weeds next to a dilapidated villa, old dog houses and garden furniture piled up in a corner, covered in blankets and rugs.

So the name for the season was never given to either of us, although it most rightly should have been given to her, I having abandoned the place and only left little bits, she having deposited all of herself there, in piles and fake deep telephone voices. But no one ever gave it to us, and we never found it, as something to roll around on our tongues; to let us, too, savor its sweetness in our mouths, to own the smell of the mud as the earth's rotation brings us closer to the sun; no one ever told us of, or referred to this season as an "ours," and let us in on whatever it is called, this "in between" winter and spring. And even if we were friends, or supposed friends, and even if we celebrated together and got lost together and had fights and made up and shared the fear of being found out and the warmth of nostalgia, even if they did say it when we were around, then it was along the lines of "this is our name, what we call our season," keeping their tongues firmly wrapped around it, this season when the tourists leave, when they get ready to let out their chickens to run around the front yard, and hang out the heavy blankets on the rails of the balconies of their ancient homes and when we are no longer really there. The word and the season, deep inside the dark hallways, far away, coveted like a pet name used for a lover, which no one else has a right to, which no one would ever dare let roll off of their own strange tongue.

When someone has a stroke, their brain has to find new pathways to make their body move. New pathways. New routines.

So *brav*. So *brav*, she throws the dog something that looks like a bone. The dog grasps it in its teeth and chews. Grind on it. I hear you.

## Pizza with Pineapple and Corn
## Lisa Rosenblatt

Sara Beth grew up in Italy. Not as in the kind of growing up that involves going to school and getting pimples. What I mean is that she became truly grown, fully grown. Specifically, it happened at a café in Venice. She'd taken the train from Vienna to Rome to meet her parents who had flown in from Cincinnati. She didn't meet them as in, "hello, nice to meet you," as she'd already met them before, after all, at the hospital in Cincinnati, when she came screaming out of her mother's womb.

So, it was many years later, around forty or so, after that first birth meeting that they met in Rome and travelled together by train, or maybe Sara Beth gave in and they took a rental car to Venice. And there in Venice, while sitting very casually at a café, letting a light breeze creep underneath their T-shirts, all three equally in need of a rest, Sara Beth's feet suddenly burst the seams of her handmade leather shoes. Sara Beth thought, maybe sneakers are more practical, but these are fine shoes, and they must have burst because of all the walking I've done. They'd started their walk at 7 a.m., and had looked at all the sights that have to be looked at so that one could say for sure that they'd been in Venice, and Sara Beth had told her parents all about her punk band and her English students, and at the Ponte di Rialto, she had turned to her mom and asked if she had ever worn black underwear, which they'd never talked about while walking down the streets of their own home town. All of that walking and talking can most definitely make feet swell.

But it wasn't just her feet. Her right hand, in an awkward attempt to reach down for her left foot, swiftly toppled a cappuccino at the next table as her arm had already nearly tripled in length. The tripling of her arm was actually a good thing, because otherwise, how else would she reach her mouth, which was nearly parallel with the minute hand of the clock on the tower pointing to half past two.

For what seemed like an eternity, but was probably only thirty seconds or so, Sara Beth could not figure out how to open her lips to say sorry (about the cappuccino) and had to use her fingers to manually pry them apart, not only to speak, but to breathe. Her mom began laughing hysterically, nearly choking on her laughter, gasping and sobbing. Sara Beth couldn't be sure if it was because of the cappuccino, a joke someone had just told, or something else entirely, as the sudden spurt in body mass had made her forget nearly every facet of the conversation they had been having up to that point.

Whatever it was that had tickled her mom's fancy, Sara Beth joined her in a cautious giggle that grew, as she had, to a deep resounding laugh, a guffaw, fits of snorts and dribble, poking at each other and waving of hands, which eventually, even though her mind had finally connected with her lips, set her gasping for air with tears streaming down, landing in huge plops on the piazza. While Sara Beth and her mom were enjoying this long belly laugh, which was incredibly damaging to the surroundings due to her size, Sara Beth's dad just kept eating his pizza. "Best pizza I ever had," he said, but Sara Beth noticed a twinkle in his eye. Like all of us, he was certainly relieved. After all, it had been a long time coming.

# Intervention
## Dan Keeble

The surf giggles childlike up the sand, clawing its way back through the pebbles, spent. The aspiration of the ocean, struggling to exhale, mimics the ventilators that were once only background noise. No longer will I be able to ignore their presence.

I am walking the path of those I have comforted. Listened to the echo of my own words. Seen for the first time the brand names of machines that relatives identify with the domestic side of that electronic business. The ovens and refrigerators. Machines that cosset their lives, now fighting to save their loved ones - until I tell them it is time to stop.

I drag a bench down the beach. It bears a dedication plaque, to someone *forever connected to the ocean*.

The two woolen blankets I drape over her limp frame pull Marianne's shoulders forward, preserving her ebbing warmth. She leans against me, drained.

Why did they use an administrator to remind me I could not treat her? It was not necessary. I knew the rules. Yet still I studied every nurse and colleague who touched her. Each silent intervention and sympathetic hand on my shoulder intensified my suffering.

The dying hours of the warm September evening is calming. To the east, the soft cliff face yields to the sea. A few trees, blackened in silhouette, lie lifeless on the sand beneath a crumbling overhang. Arteries of black-thorn roots, exposed by erosion, are clinging on hopelessly in the face of inevitability.

Is it twenty, thirty, fifty times I have hardened to relatives pleading? Now I am haunted by my responses: *Let her go peacefully. Moving her can only add to her stress. Why give dad further discomfort?* They were right to beg. *But, I want to take him home.* I don't want him to die here. Recalling their gnawing desperation, I am ashamed.

Marianne's shallow breathing synchronises with the ocean. Thirty-seven year old lungs fighting with race-end exhaustion. The slightest witness of a smile grows at the corner of her colourless lips. I feel she is content, aware I have brought her to our place.

Sixteen hours from the end of all intervention. At 2 am. the nurses abandon their station to deal with some emergency. Empty corridors. Nobody would challenge a doctor wheeling a patient away. Away from the harsh lights and sterile beeping. Colleagues will struggle to understand. But, I have learned understanding and feeling are oceans apart.

Now, on the beach, the contrast is immeasurable. The slow-sinking sun drives warm golden leaves of wavelets towards us. Her eyes are open, although I am uncertain whether she drinks the view. Pulses of gentle breeze brush her eyelashes and lift small wisps of dull auburn hair above her ear. Never has there been such closeness. Never has there been such happiness. The universe awaits with empathy.

I cuddle her head to my chest and allow the blankets to cocoon us. One final kiss on her forehead. A shiver. Then we watch the sun disappear into the ocean, and wait until she is forever cold.

# THE FORCE
## Jean Ende

Good Lord, you look just like Yoda!

Probably not the best thing to say when someone pulls off her wig to show you the effects of their chemotherapy. But that's what I said.

After years of listening to my cousin Amy complain about the size of her ears (which were generally hidden under long hair in continually changing shades of red and blond) it turns out that those ears really are enormous. Just like the ones the Star Wars icon has. And they stick-out. Way out. Like they're trying to flee the balding skull that's clinging to a few remaining wisps of pale brown hair.

"Those are the longest earlobes I've ever seen," I said. "Why didn't you get your ears done when we were all getting our noses fixed?"

"Because my parents wouldn't pay for two procedures," she said. "I could hide my ears, but a nose is always right out there for everyone to see."

"That makes sense, although I never thought your nose really needed work."

I stepped closer to get a better view of her ears. "They're not pierced," I said. "I don't know anyone who graduated from college in the '70s with virginal lobes."

"Well I didn't want to attract attention to them."

"Why not get them done now?" I said. "Go get dressed."

I was hoping that once she got out of the floor-length flannel nightgown in which she'd answered the door I'd be able to stop thinking about the tiny Jedi warrior. Somehow without her hair Amy seemed smaller. Could cancer treatment make you shorter? Was it the illness, age, or just my perception?

Amy was my older cousin, five years older. She was a relative on my mother's side, didn't live near us in the Bronx so I didn't see her as often as the cousins on my father's side who were neighbors. Growing up she'd always been too big to play with me, too far ahead, too far away. Eventually I'd caught up and we became close, shared memories of Aunt Gussie and Uncle Harry and their eerie old house.

"I'll treat you to a pair of genuine hippie earrings," I said. "The kind our parents wouldn't have allowed us to wear."

Of course the first jeweler we approached took one look at Amy, her pale skin and missing eyebrows, and explained that the slight chance of infection from even the most sanitary ear piercing made it a bad idea for someone whose body was being bombarded by poisonous chemicals.

"You come back when you're healthy and I'll pierce your ears for half price," he said, patting her thin hand. "And throw in a pair of solid gold studs."

Anyway, by that time I'd remembered that you can't wear dangling earrings for at least a few months after the piercing and it didn't seem like a good idea to make long-range plans with Amy. I bought her a pair of shiny clip-on hoops studded with bright aqua stones. They weren't real gold and I worried that they'd turn her earlobes green.

"If that happens I'm going to blame it on the radiation and demand that the doctor reimburse me," she said. But within an hour she'd taken them off because the earrings were too tight and were giving her a headache.

I never saw the earrings again but I don't regret the purchase. That was one of the last times Amy and I spent an afternoon just being silly. We'd spent the previous months crying together, trying to find an interpretation for the doctor's words that provided any believable encouragement. We eventually decided we were tired of always being sad, and we were out of tissues. We went to a large department store and sprayed each other with perfume and tried on expensive fur coats the salespeople knew we wouldn't buy.

By early afternoon Amy was tired and I was hungry. We went to a local luncheonette and she immediately left to use the bathroom.

"I'll have my usual," she said, leaving me to explain to the waiter that she wanted an extra tall glass of ginger ale with at least four maraschino cherries in it. That had been her order at the diner our parents took us to on Sunday afternoons when we were little. I don't know how they make maraschino cherries these days but I figured a little bit of red dye #2 wouldn't hurt now.

"I'll decide what else I want went I get back," she said. "Maybe I'll just have some of yours. Get something good."

By the time Amy returned to the table the waiter had brought the order. She was paler than she'd been previously. Amy drank half of her soda, nibbled on one of my French fries and said she was tired and wanted to go home. I didn't say anything, just paid the check and hailed a cab.

A month later she was in a hospice where they gave her a soft flannel turban so her now totally bald head wouldn't be cold. It covered her ears. A few weeks later she was gone.

###

# Train
## Elana Gomel

Crawling in the thick darkness, Daniel was brought short by a blow to the head and instinctively lashed out.

His fist connected with something rotten-soft. Warm wetness splattered his fingers.

The car had been quiet at first but now a chorus of groans, cries and indignant exclamations was beginning to rise, a swelling music of fear.

He had been tossed onto the floor by a series of convulsions that shook the train after the lights went out. Somebody landed on top of him, a child by the weight of her, shaking and sobbing. He tried to comfort her, but she rolled off him and disappeared into the stifling darkness.

At least she could cry. Judging by the inert bodies he kept bumping into not every one of the passengers had been so lucky.

He tried to stand up, but his legs gave way. He gritted his teeth and crawled forward, a tiny insignificant parasite inside the body of a giant.

Something tickled the back of his head. It was a gentle tentative touch, almost caressing. He brushed it away, but it came back, more insistent that time.

He brushed it off again. His right hand was caught, pulled back and up, held at an unnatural angle to his body. He yelped and tugged at the restraint. The derma loop tightened around his wrist, cutting off circulation.

He hauled himself up, using the restraint as the leverage. His head hit the ribbed ceiling. He staggered but was held upright by the loop that was gradually pulling his arm away from him, threatening to wrench it out of its socket.

How could this be? The height of the car was enough to give ample clearance even to a man much taller than himself.

Who was he fooling? He knew exactly how this could be.

"Shut up, all of you!" Daniel yelled. "Shut up and listen!"

His voice rose above the hubbub of children's crying, adults' sobbing, confused unanswered questions flung into the void. Some woman's piercing voice was repeating a single syllable: a name? And underneath this babel of fear was the cause of it all: a whispering uninterrupted purl like a soft leakage of some viscous fluid from a giant open valve.

Daniel wanted to scream. The pain in his twisted arm was bad and growing worse as the contracting muscles of the loop inexorably pulled it up and back, forcing him to stretch until he was standing on his tiptoes, his head pressed against the ribbed ceiling. He groped in darkness with his free hand, trying to reach the base of the loop but his fingers fell short just a couple of centimeters.

He let the scream come out as a commanding shout.

The volume of noise dropped down a notch.

"Stop panicking!" he yelled. "You're making it worse! Help is on the way! Just stop moving around, hunker down where you are, and keep quiet! I repeat: don't move around, don't make a sound if you want to live!"

This got their attention.

"Who are you?" a cranky old man's voice snapped at him. And overlaying it, a woman's voice, as clear and familiar as an alarm bell: "What's happening?"

The train is going rogue," he replied and instantly regretted his truthfulness as the voices erupted once again in a cacophony of horror.

"Shut up!" he bellowed again. "I'm a militiaman; I know how to deal with this! We'll be just fine as long as we don't whet his appetite! He feels live prey moving in his belly, he'll crank up stomach juice so much that we'll all be crap before you finish crapping your pants!"

A couple of gasps but the shuffle of movements went down. Daniel bit his lip, tried to pivot around so as to relieve pressure on his shoulder. His left hand brushed the back of a seat and he winced: it was as soft as a rotting fruit and feverishly hot; the tiny vibrissae that should have been lying down to form the plush cover were all standing up agitatedly. A stinging wetness clung to his fingertips. He swore and waved the hand in the air, trying to shake off the acidic juice. He hit a weave of fabric that was so inert it must be a person's clothes. And then something clamped onto his free wrist, something that was not the guts of the train, and a voice whispered into his ear, so close that a warm breath ruffled his hair:

"Daniel!"

He jerked and cursed as the loop tightened again, cutting off the circulation even further. His hand felt like a blood-swollen balloon.

"Who's this?"
"Kora."
"Who the fuck are you?"

The person recoiled but now he could smell her: soap and shampoo and underneath it the heady, musky aroma of a woman.

"Never mind," he whispered through gritted teeth. "Help me get free. We have to get the hell out of here!"
"But help…"
"If they were to come, they would be here already!"

Amazingly, she did not flinch; she was so close to him that he could feel the swell of her breasts and the rapid beating of her heart.

"What can I do?"
"Feel up my right arm…careful…yes. Can you feel it?"
"The loop?"
"Squeeze it hard at the base…yes. Harder. They have a reflex. If you do it right, they'll relax."

Her body pressed against his, her arm sliding across his face.

"Yes, like this. Careful, don't let it loop you instead."

He heard a hiss somewhere close in this dense darkness filled with the smells and whimpering of frightened people and the stink of the rising gastric tide. The loop tightened so much he was afraid his wrist-bones would snap.

And then it relaxed and he was free.

He jerked forward, almost bringing her down, but she balanced herself somehow.

"Don't touch anything!" he hissed. "Especially the seats and the loops! And keep to the aisle!"

The darkness was so absolute he imagined his eyes had turned around, looking inside his skull. He blinked a couple of times, just to reassure himself it was not so. Was the entire system affected? Was the underground maze of MTT now a skein of lightless tunnels prowled by rogue trains?

Something splattered him, a spray of liquid from above, and there was a star map of stinging points on his face and bare neck. A child's voice wailed in the dark:

"Mummy, it burns!"

He put his hands onto the woman's shoulders, turned her around, so the swish of her long hair momentarily cooled the acid-burns on his face.

"There is a door about five seats from where we are," he whispered. "Go ahead. Then turn right."

He felt her nod and then she moved on and he followed, his right hand securely clamped on her shoulder, her fresh smell overpowered by the meaty stink of the train's gastric juices.

"Get up from the seats but don't move!" he yelled. "Don't move! I'll try to open the door!"

A scream, then another. A woman's frantic voice:

"My son…the seat won't let him up!"

Kora – if this was her name – bumped into somebody and he was brought up short, bumping into her. It would be funny – were it not for the fact that they were about to be digested by the train like a bunch of fucking zombies!

He still could not quite believe it was happening.

"Where do you think you're going?"

She just shoved the owner of the gruff voice out of the way. Daniel felt the swell of her muscles and the ease with which she cut through the press of bodies in the aisle.

A leathery tentacle whipped across his face. He pushed it aside and heard a gasp as it fastened around somebody else's throat, a death rattle of suffocation that was quickly drowned in the rhythmical puffing that now permeated the car. The walls, the floor, the ceiling throbbed in unison, releasing gouts of acid that flew through the shrinking cavity. The hand-straps thrashed around, catching people's arms, legs, and heads in their leathery embrace. Ducking and weaving in the dark, the panicky passengers congealed into a single hydra-like body, blindly flailing around, as the eager mouths opening in the swollen seats and dripping walls took bites out of them.

## Transformation
## Katie Keridan

It's so very dark in here.

Normally, I'm not bothered by darkness, sometimes even preferring it to the blinding light of day, but right now, at this particular moment, I miss the sun. I miss the warmth, the expansiveness, the confidence that comes with movement and action. Or at least knowing that I *could* move and act, if I so chose.

But I left all that behind when I decided to come here…when I willingly surrendered my freedom and entered this confinement of darkness and solitude. I am certain it will be for my betterment, although I don't know when or even how.

All I know is that I seek transformation, and this is the path to it. If change means perpetual night, I will wrap myself in darkness. If becoming who I was meant to be requires stillness, I will learn to stop moving. If achieving the dream I so desperately desire means giving up every last vestige of myself, I will cast it all away, shed the too-small skin of yesterday, and become something new, something different, something totally unrecognizable compared to the creature I was.

And so, I wait.

Sometimes, I wait patiently; most times; I do not. *Is it time? Has it been long enough? How will I know when the transformation is complete?*

Doubt sets in. *Did I really think this was the best way to achieve my dream?*

Insecurity follows swiftly behind. *Who am I to undertake such a radical change? Surely those better or smarter or stronger than me have attempted such a thing with far less impressive results…why do I believe I can succeed where they failed?*

Anger quickly appears, jostling its way to the forefront. *It's not fair! Why is it taking so long when I already worked so hard?*

Over anger's fury, I hear the soft voice of sadness. *What did I do wrong? Why do I want these things if I'm not meant to have them?*

I reassert the need to be patient, even as I wiggle and shift and squint to see if I've missed anything. She told me this would happen, I remind myself. She told me this was not for the faint of heart. She said it would cost everything, and I agreed it was worth it.

I replay her words, reassuring myself: *"You cannot look deeply into yourself without being changed; this is why so few willingly choose to face their own darkness. But those who do so will be transformed."*

For a while, I feel better. Calmer, more secure in the decision I made.

And then, doubt creeps in, and the cycle begins all over again.

*I will die here*, I think one day after who knows how long. *I will die, without success, without becoming who I dreamed of being, and without living the life I imagined the Universe wanted for me. I will die unloved, forgotten, and getting exactly what I deserved for daring to think I could change who I am.*

Just when I can stand it no long, I hear something…distant words that I cannot make out…a voice, moving closer…

"Poniniyku, puuhu –
Awaken, recently made."

And then suddenly, there is light, the smallest sliver, but so bright to eyes accustomed to the dark that I cringe away even as my heart beats faster.

*Is this it? Can this truly be happening?*

The light expands, chasing away the shadows that have been my constant, and only, companions for so long, shrinking the blackness, until all I see is the golden sunlight pouring in, bathing me, warming me from the inside out. I lean towards it, then fall forward, unable to stop myself from tumbling out of the sticky, silky chrysalis.

Thankfully, I fall right into her outstretched hand.

As if she knew I would be weak and need help.

I stumble for a moment, unused to this new body, working to get my legs beneath me. Blinking, I finally manage to stand and lift my gaze. She bows her head in reverence, then smiles, blinking warm brown eyes at me.

"Welcome," says the Butterfly Maiden. "You have been transformed. Tell me, what did you find in your darkness?"

I tentatively move first one wing, then the other, marveling at the swirls of black and orange that appear to have been painted on the gossamer filaments that are now a part of me. I dreamed of flight for so long, and now I can take to the skies whenever I want. My amazement makes it difficult to focus on the Butterfly Maiden's question, but I do my best to redirect my attention.

"I learned many things," I reply, "chief of which is that I am not patient, regardless of the body I am in."

She nods in acknowledgement. Sunlight glints off her wings, beautiful stained-glass creations that are taller than she is and shimmer with abstract patterns of reds, greens, blues, and yellows.

"I never actually felt myself changing," I admitted. "Time ran together, and I saw no evidence of growth. But then, after days and days of feeling as if nothing was happening, it's as if everything happened all at once, and now, I find myself completely transformed."

The Butterfly Maiden nods. "Stillness is not the same as stagnation."

I flutter my wings and begin to rise off the Butterfly Maiden's palm.

"Be who you were meant to be," she whispers, and I rise, boosted by a gentle wind, exulting in the wings I wept, dreamed, and hoped for, and head off to discover who I have now become.

## Pretty Flamingo
### William John Rostron

"Pretty Flamingo." It was a catchy tune by Manfred Mann that seemed to be in my head on that summer day in 1966. Maria was scheduled to move the next morning. Though there was sadness in me that day, an all-consuming anger was my most dominant emotion. The band saw this and knew that I needed a break.

We'd all given up our summer jobs and were practicing almost eight hours a day. For most of the summer Maria and I had found a way to be together before, after, and sometimes even during practices. However, in the last week, her parents demanded that she stay home and pack. The band all liked Maria, so on that last day, we broke practice early so that I could be with her.

As the sun was setting over our Cambria Heights neighborhood, I ran over to Maria's house. However, her father refused to let her come outside. He had never really liked me and was trying to end it right there and then. I could hear Maria begging her father to let her out, but it was to no avail. Her father still held it against me that my family had not joined them in the "white flight" that had consumed our neighborhood. In his eyes, we were fools for not joining what had now become a full-blown Causcasian stampede.

As I stood outside Maria's house, my fury grew and I wanted to strike out at someone or something. I wouldn't hurt a living person with my temper. However, inanimate objects were fair game.

Like so many other front yards in the Heights, the amount of grass was so minuscule that it could be "mowed" in fifteen minutes using only a pair of scissors. This made it doubly confusing that people chose to decorate these small patches of green with really cheap ornaments. The most common of these adornments were plastic pink flamingos. I still don't understand the reason for an ugly tropical bird decorating a lawn in New York City. However, they were in abundance in my neighborhood, including the one that I had chosen to strangle in frustration that very afternoon. In the midst of my attempted murder of the plastic flamingo, Maria's mother came out of the house. As a feeble explanation, I blurted out, "The flamingo started it." She looked at me like I was nuts and asked me emphatically to leave. I was furious but realized that any answer I gave would only cause more problems. Frustrated, I looked back at the flamingo, and in a soft voice, uttered, "This isn't over."

I returned to see if the guys wanted to resume practice, but only Jimmy and Gio were still there. As I told my story, they both tried to calm me down. They were right. We left the basement for fear my verbal outrage would offend Jimmy's parents. Once out in the street and a safe distance away, I let loose with a stream of obscenities that didn't end until we had traveled almost to the eastern border of the Heights. Knowing my pain, they just let me go on. Ironically, when I finally stopped ranting, I found myself standing next to, of all things, another plastic flamingo.

"Screw you, and your smiley pink face too," I remember saying to the flamingo that was taunting me. Apparently, in my mind, he had spoken with the other plastic bird on the flamingo hotline. Gio laughed and then broke into a chorus of "Pretty Flamingo," and Jimmy was soon harmonizing with him. My anger came down a notch or two. I had a plan.

Jimmy, Gio, and I never slept that night. In the Great Flamingo Round-up of 1966, the three of us found every flamingo that had been bought by the evil flamingo slaveholders of the Heights. After requisitioning three shopping carts from a supermarket, we systematically scoured the streets for our prey.

By four in the morning, we were pretty sure that we had herded all the stray flamingos from the entire area into our wagon train. We then had the first and only flamingo drive in recorded history. They arrived at their final destination a little before sunrise. We quietly placed the more than three-dozen plastic birds on the Romano family lawn. When every inch of the grass was covered with our pink friends, we filled the concrete, railing, and exterior walls with the overflow birds. We would have liked to have stayed and watched their reaction but thought better about being caught *pink-handed*.

In my anger, I had only hurt myself. I couldn't go say goodbye to Maria as her family prepared to leave the next day. Even so, there was great satisfaction in knowing that we had reunited an entire tribe of birds that had so long been separated by man's inhumanity to his plastic brothers.

## Chapter 23: Violet
## Helen Aitchison

Crematorium

'For the love of God Violet, do you have to bloody cremate everything?'

Violet sat across the table, barely four feet apart yet his words didn't even register. She had stopped trying to listen to Ben a long time ago. She heard every word, but listening was pointless. She could never win and words always meant something different each time they poured out of his abhorrent mouth. Violet had been on the receiving end of 'not listening' dozens of times over the years. Now, it was like her spirit couldn't stand listening anymore, as her soul slowly eroded like cliffs from the salty sea.

'I followed the instructions Ben, mine is fine', she said in deflated monotone.

'Well you must be stupid as well as useless then' he sneered.

'How am I meant to eat this pig swill when you could tarmac roads with it'?

He picked up his plate and even though she knew what was going to happen, she made no attempts to avoid it.

Smash and splat. The sounds, the sensations. She had heard, felt, saw, and smelt this event so many times before. Another plate broken on the floor. Another pile of food, smeared onto the beautiful porcelain kitchen floor tiles. More brown marks splattered up the white paintwork, more sprays of food landing on Violet. Her face, clothes, and hair full of raindrops of gravy and herbs.

Strange how she had stopped flinching as much, as the pain became so much more than physical. This had led to more abuse. She would receive the odd kick, pushing her off the dining table chair, a quick hair pull as he stormed off, a push against a piece of heavy furniture. Yet her body, just like the not listening, had stopped reacting like it used to. Was it giving up? Maybe. Was it just her becoming accustomed to the behaviour? Most likely. Or was it because her heart that once felt filled with love and hope, felt torn and dead.

Flinching, crying, pleading, speaking, it never changed anything.

She hated this man, this bastard man. This cruel, spiteful, abusive excuse of a man. She hated him with every cell in her body and prayed he would have a heart attack at work.
That he would die and be eradicated from her existence. That his sick, vindictive, perverted, sinister heart would explode and he would be gone. God, did she pray.

'No other man would put up with you Vi, you're a complete nightmare, the lads all think it. Always moaning, bloody nagging. And you're a lazy bitch, sponging off me instead of working full time. Aye, you are bloody lucky to have me Vi. I suggest you be a little bit more damn grateful that I put up with you and put food on this table.'

And on that parade of verbal diarrhoea, Ben got up and left, heading down the local pub as he did 8 out of 10 times he had a go. The other 2, didn't end that way.

Violet sat and sobbed. She cried for the monster Ben had become, when 12 years earlier, he had been a gentleman, courting her and charming her. She cried for the doormat she had become, the target, 'that woman' who puts up with anything. She cried because she needed a way out, but had no energy, her mind too depleted to think of options. She cried because she was only 31 years old and felt 91.

That night she cried, with no idea that the next day would be the start of her new chapter.

# Company
## A.O. Wallat

Gordon sauntered along the giant green bamboo that he had decided was his favourite viewing spot. The landscape never changed from other vantages but at ninth hour the light from where he now stood streaked through the canopy turning the dull wooden city into the many shades of sunset.

Although the cityscape reflected reds and yellows quite cheerfully he didn't feel the same. Sad wasn't exactly what he felt because he never felt it like this before. The wooden folk were always too busy to think or even worse talk about feelings.

Gordon sat down with a clunk. The giant bamboo had no back rest and he clearly forgot about that. His wooden frame tumbled backwards from the canopy end after end, clonk after clunk and with a dull thud he hit the floor. His bark was split, his head was cracked. Little pieces of splinter embedded the soil and all manner of sap was dripping on his head.

Gordon woke in pain. Wincing, he crawled towards the nearest tree as though an anchor weighed him down. He had no memory of the moments just passed and looked down in search of the missing time.

Fear trickled down into the pit of his stomach.

Two standard log lengths before him was another body slumped in the same way he was. It looked just as broken as he did. In fact he looked exactly the same. Bathed in an orange glow, the two Gordons sat facing each other. He wasn't sure if he was dead. But when Gordon tried to leave –

"Don't go," it said.

Its frame hadn't moved, its eyes didn't move but it had definitely spoken.

The shadows turned from orange to red. Gordon had managed to sit upright. While he rested, the sap in his cracks and breaks hardened and slowly healed. He looked at his double. The corners of its mouth were turned down. Gordon spoke without thinking.

"Come on. Let's get home."

# Life-Marks
## Christy O'Callaghan-Leue

"It's embarrassing," I tell my boyfriend Mark as he slides his left pointer finger emblazoned with blue letters spelling "last straw" across my ribs. He says it makes him feel like a cradle robber to look at my flawless dermis.

"I'm waiting for the cops to drag me away," he drawls with a sly smile, a pierced eyebrow raised.

I can stand naked in front of the mirror and inspect my body for an hour at a time, a frown on my soft pink lips. I'm smooth as cream, not so much as a blemish, a freckle, or a scar. Twenty-eight-years-old and I'm the only one I know with glowing, dewy skin.

My best friend Stacy's first one appear when she was five and her mom died. A teddy bear holding a heart was on her left shoulder the next time I saw her at school. It was followed by a broken arrow along the inside of her right thigh when our JV soccer coach forced his purple-stained fingers inside her after practice.

There's hardly any open space on Mark's thirty-year-old body. His first one appeared when he was seven and fell off the rope swing at a lake, a cartoonish dive-bombing duck on his right butt cheek where he landed on the rocks. Some of his life-marks have started to fade. As we huddle naked under the ivory Egyptian cotton sheets of my bed, he wonders aloud if new ones will take their place as he gets older.

"Luck doesn't go my way," he says then breathes in the honeysuckle scent of my hair.

As we lay with our legs intertwined, I search his colors and shapes, pointing to the bleeding hearts on his left peck, the clown with the razor-sharp teeth on his calf, the trumpet on his forearm, and ask for the story that created the image. I kiss the ones that were sad and lick the happy ones. Then place his fingers with the words "love me" inside my mouth, the bitter sting of nicotine spreads across my tongue.

I set up my camera on a tripod. The remote hidden in my hand as I pose flesh against flesh, his so busy and loud and mine so silent and spare. I click the shutter.

My photos of skin have been featured in magazines, on websites, even in ad campaigns. My following on Instagram is massive, but I have to be careful not to get censored for showing the occasional nipple. The photos hang in galleries and shops across the country. My dull, nude body is my most common subject since I'm readily available. I am my own best seller. People love a freak. However, I prefer the visual essay of other people's landscapes—their life written across their beautiful patchwork membrane.

I let out a giggle as Mark runs his lips down my spine. He stops and pulls me upright. "Holy shit, babe."

"What's up?"

"Your back." The heat from his stare radiates across my shell, sending goosebumps down my arms.

"What is it?"

"I've never seen it happened before. Mine always appear while I'm sleeping." He snaps a pic with his phone and turns the screen towards me. A snowy peaked mountain range full of grays, purples, blues, and greens runs from shoulder blade to shoulder blade. I throw his phone, cracking the screen, and scream for him to leave until he shrugs into his clothes and slams the door.

I haven't slept nor eaten since Mark left. It's been twenty hours. My phone's off. Not sure I want to know whatever created that graffiti on my marble flesh. Every drop of envy for other people's stories drained from my heart. Such an idiot I'd convinced myself I was special, somehow immune. With my exposed back in front of the lens, my thumb clicks the remote. I drag my sweatshirt over my shoulders and check the shot, hoping the vandalism has disappeared.

*Telemachus Triumphs*
Mark Blickley

WALLY LEGGIT---- A recently retired bus driver, 65, quite out of shape

MYRTLE LEGGIT--- A slim, athletic woman, 60, married to Wally.

*The curtain opens on a very neat, very masculine study. Stage right is the doorway entrance to the study where we see WALLY seated in a stylish desk chair that he slowly wheels over to his desk. The chair seems to be attached to him as he kicks out his legs to gain momentum and direction; in fact, he could almost pass for a strange new kind of insect. WALLY could leave the chair any time he wishes, but he has no desire to. He's a perfect example of inertia in motion. When WALLY reaches the desk he pulls a large World Atlas out of a drawer and begins to thumb through it. Suddenly we hear a woman's scream. His wife, MYRTLE, bursts into the room on roller skates, holding a cage.*

### MYRTLE
He's dead! He's dead! Telemachus is dead! He's dead, Wally! Telemachus is dead!
*(WALLY grabs the cage, examines it)* I was watching him running the wheel like he always does, like he loves to do, and the just sort of squealed and flopped over. I can't believe Telemachus is dead.

### WALLY
*(examines gerbil with his finger)*
He's gone.

### MYRTLE
Oh, Wally, it's so cruel. He was the sweetest gerbil we ever had. How could he leave us?

### WALLY
*(upset)*
I don't know, Myrtle. I don't know! You say he was on his wheel when it happened?

### MYRTLE
*(nods)*
He was hitting such a graceful stride when it……..

*(MYRTLE covers her face with her hands as WALLY pulls out the tiny odometer attached to the wheel)*

### WALLY
My God, look at these figures! Telemachus put three tenths of a mile on his odometer since I checked it last night.

### MYRTLE
You can't be serious. Let me see. *(she skates over to Wally)*

### WALLY
*(visibly shaken)*
It's not fair! He had so much further to go. *(Pause)* I guess the little fellow went out in his prime, hitting his stride. You can't ask for a more noble death.

### MYRTLE
What? Spinning himself into a grave is a noble death?

### WALLY
Why can't you offer me some comfort? I loved Telemachus much more than you'll ever know.

*(MYRTLE skates up behind WALLY and puts her arms around his neck)*

**MYRTLE**

Yes, I know.

**WALLY**

I felt…..I felt as if you'd given birth to him, Myrtle, that he was really my son.

**MYRTLE**

Oh, Wally, that's disgusting.

**WALLY**

How can you call love disgusting?

**MYRTLE**

Love's not disgusting but the papers on the bottom of his cage are. If you felt so strongly about Telemachus how come I always had to change the papers?

**WALLY**

He was my baby, my baby. I always thought of him as a tiny Rumplestiltskin, majestically at his wheel, spinning out golden love.

**MYRTLE**

He did have a rather strong smell, Wally.

**WALLY**
*(in tears)*

He was a good boy. A hard working boy.

**MYRTLE**

But he never got anywhere, Wally. Do you think Telemachus lived a full life?

**WALLY**
*(jolted)*

Of course he did! What kind of nonsense are you talking?

**MYRTLE**

He lived in a cage, Wally.

**WALLY**

So?

**MYRTLE**

He lived in a cage and ran around in circles.

**WALLY**

Why are you being so cruel? What was the alternative? Have you forgotten the time you set him loose in the garden?

**MYRTLE**
*(shivers)*

I… I don't want to think about it.

**WALLY**
*(holds the cage up to her face)*

Look at him! Look at the boy! Yes, he lived in a cage. Yes, he ran day and night on his wheel. But what happened the time you decided to give him his freedom? The day you put him next to the cucumbers and told him he was free?

**MYRTLE**
*(shaking)*

I….I don't remember. Leave me alone, Wally. I don't want to think about it.

*(MYRTLE grabs for the cage; WALLY pulls it away)*

**WALLY**
*(angrily)*

What happened to Telemachus the day you locked him out of his cage?

**MYRTLE**
*(holds up her arm as if fending off a blow)*

He……squealed.

**WALLY**

That's right. And what else did he do?

**MYRTLE**

He peed on the turnips.

**WALLY**

That's right. And what else did he do?

*(At this point MYRTLE is skating around the room as WALLY chases after her in his desk chair)*

**MYRTLE**

I don't remember.

**WALLY**
*(like a petulant child)*

What else did he do? What did he do? What did he do? What did he do? What did he do?

**MYRTLE**
*(spins, faces Wally)*

He….ran away from me.

**WALLY**

That's right. And when was the next time you saw him?

**MYRTLE**

Stop it, Wally. Stop it! It's too horrible!

**WALLY**

Myrtle! When was the next time you saw Telemachus!

*(MYRTLE breaks into tears and puts her head in WALLY's lap)*

**MYRTLE**

The next time I saw him was down the road by the Flanagan property.

**WALLY**

And where was he?

**MYRTLE**

I told you. At the Flanagan's.

**WALLY**

Where was Telemachus, Myrtle?

*(MYRTLE jumps to her feet, skates over to a corner and screams)*

**MYRTLE**

He was inside! He was inside their Great Dane's mouth!

**WALLY**

That's right! He was being chewed up by the Flanagan dog. And you called it freedom! You called it a gift!

**MYRTLE**
*(near tears)*

How did I know he……

**WALLY**
*(interrupts, wheels over to her)*

I rescued him. I gave Telemachus a second chance at life! *(MYRTLE is crying)* He had a quality existence. Telemachus had love, security, food, clean papers. But more important he had a purpose, a mission. He had motion!

**MYRTLE**

But he never got anywhere, Wally. He just went around in circles.

**WALLY**

What's wrong with circles? What shape is your wedding ring?

**MYRTLE**
*(looks at hand)*

A circle.

**WALLY**

That's right. Don't you understand when Telemachus traveled in a circle he viewed life at every possible angle?

**MYRTLE**

You know, I never thought of it like that.

**WALLY**

It's true. I made that discovery way back during my professional driving test, when they made me do figure eights with the bus. You see, driving a bus was not only a career, but an education.

**MYRTLE**

You have such a brilliant, Walter Leggit. Are you ashamed of having me as a wife? Am I too dull?

**WALLY**
*(kisses her)*

What, are you kidding? Any woman who can produce such offspring *(He holds up cage)* is worth her weight in gold, Rumplestiltskin or no Rumplestiltskin. And speaking of golden rumps…… *(He squeezes Myrtle's behind)*

**MYRTLE**
*(giggles, pulls his hand away)*

Stop that! Don't be so fresh in front of Telemachus. He's still warm yet.

*(WALLY gazes at the cage and gently pats it)*

**WALLY**

Telemachus was all man. He'd have understood. *(Pause)* I miss him. I miss my baby, sweetheart.

**MYRTLE**

We can get another pet, Wally.

**WALLY**
*(sighs)*

I suppose so. But can he be replaced?

**MYRTLE**

Oh, come on, Wally. Telemachus is the seventh gerbil we've had in the past three years.

**WALLY**
*(shakes head)*

Yes, but none of them racked up the mileage old Telemachus did. I guess the little darlings are built for speed, not endurance. I'll pick up his successor tomorrow morning.

**MYRTLE**

Wally……

**WALLY**
*(in deep thought)*

Yes?

**MYRTLE**

Dear….

**WALLY**

What is it?

**MYRTLE**

Honey, do we have to get another rodent? Can't we get a dog or a cat this time?

**WALLY**

Absolutely not!

**MYRTLE**
*(getting angry)*

Why not? Why can't I have a pet I can pick up and hug? What's wrong with a cat?

**WALLY**

They're lazy. They sleep twenty hours a day.

**MYRTLE**

Then let's get a dog. A strong, energetic dog. They can last twenty years.

**WALLY**

Oh, great! Can't you just see us in twenty years, bent over and using a cane, walking a dog? Besides, ever since I pulled Telemachus out from the jaws of the Great Dane, I hate dogs. All they ever do is piss on your tires.

*(MYRTLE furiously skates over to WALLY and snatches the cage out of his hands)*

**MYRTLE**

I'm going to bury him in the turnip patch! *(She skates out of the room)*

*(WALLY wheels himself over to the door, cups his hand to his mouth, and calls out to his wife)*

**WALLY**

No, don't bury him there, Myrtle. Turnips grow below the ground. I don't want Telemachus sharing his space with anything else. Plant him in with the cucumbers. *(He slowly wheels himself back to his desk and shakes his head)* I guess people deal with their grief in different ways. *(Pause)* Where was I?

*(WALLY picks up his World Atlas and flips through the pages as he slowly spins in his chair. His spinning becomes faster as he excitedly turns the pages, until his chair whorls out of control and he falls off)*

CURTAIN

# *SINKING*
## *Nika Rose*

## **PROLOGUE**

*Lights up on SINKING.*
*She sits cross-legged.*
*A rope is tied around her waist.*
*An anchor is tied to the other side of the rope.*
*She sits.*
*And sits.*
*And sits.*
*Breathing.*
*She makes a move to stand.*
*Her movement is labored but she makes her way to her feet.*
*She looks.*
*Left.*
*Right.*
*She walks toward the left until she runs out of slack.*
*She pauses.*
*She walks toward the right until she runs out of slack.*
*Tethered like a dog to a lamppost.*
*She doesn't seem to acknowledge the anchor.*
*She struggles to walk.*
*Left.*
*Right.*
*Forward.*
*Backward.*
*But she can't.*
*She puts her hand to the rope around her stomach. Acknowledging it for the first time.*
*She rubs her fingers against the rough surface.*
*She pulls a few splinters out her hand.*
*She looks down to the anchor.*
*She takes a hold of the rope and drags the anchor.*
*Stepping.*
*She drags.*
*And drags.*
*She is exasperated.*
*Breathing heavily now.*
*She pauses for a moment.*
*She lets go of the rope and lets the anchor sink back into the earth.*
*She sits on top of it.*
*She catches her breath.*
*After a moment she stands.*
*She drags the anchor again.*
**Drag.**
**Drag.**
**Drag.**
*She collapses onto the ground.*
*The rope still tied around her convulsing stomach.*
*The anchor beside her.*
*She curls up into the fetal position.*
*She breathes.*
*And breathes.*

*And breathes.*
*She closes her eyes.*
*Her breath stops for a moment.*
*She opens her eyes.*
*She looks to the anchor.*
*She reaches out and touches it.*
*She rubs it.*
*Slowly.*
*Sensually.*
*Intently.*
*She pulls it closer toward her.*
*She looks at it.*
*She pulls it into her chest.*
*Cradling it.*
*They become one.*
*Time and space expand.*
*They transform into stone.*
*A statue.*
*A relic.*
*A painful moment of stillness.*

## SCENE 1

*SINKING sits alone, naked in a kiddy pool.*
*It is brimming with water.*
*A moment of stillness.*
*SWIMMING emerges from somewhere.*
*He takes in the sight.*
*Breath.*
*SWIMMING undresses and squeezes in the pool beside her.*
*The water pours over the top.*
*SINKING tries to catch the water as it escapes.*
*Cupping it with her hands.*
*She looks to SWIMMING.*

**SINKING**
Are you trying to dry me out?

**SWIMMING**
…

**SINKING**
…

*SINKING tries to pull the remaining water closer to herself. FLOATING approaches the pool from behind and does the kiddy pool equivalent of a cannonball.*
*The remaining water flies everywhere.*
*Maybe an inch at most is left.*
*They are squished in space.*
*SINKING cups little bits of water in her hands.*
*She licks it, like a cat lapping up milk.*

> *The water falls through her fingers.*
> *She looks at FLOATING incredulously.*

**SINKING**
*I guess I'll just suffocate and die.*

> *SINKING crawls out of the kiddy pool and storms off.*
> *FLOATING looks at SWIMMING.*

**SWIMMING**
*She thinks she's a fish.*

## SCENE 2

> *SINKING lays in the grass.*
> *Lightly flailing like a fish.*

**SINKING**
*Drained*
*Parched*
*Depleted*
*I'm drying out*
*My veins are drying out*
*Scratching together like sandpaper*
*I can no longer produce spit*
*I lick my fingers and can't detect a trace of moisture*
*I'm withering away*
*Evaporating*
*Desiccating*
*Desiccat-ion*
*Hydration*
*I need to hydrate*
*Hydrate my cells*
*Quench my cells*
*They would suck the water out of my cells if they could*
*They would take tiny syringes and suck out every droplet*
*They take*
*And take*
*And take*
*Until I'm ready for the gutting*
*I'm on ice in the market*
**I'm seared in a pan**
*I'm perfectly aware that I'm not actually a fish*

> *She lays.*
> *A wave of drought comes.*
> *She shrivels.*
> *She curls up into a ball.*
> *Desicates.*
> *Mummifies.*

## SCENE 3

> *Lights up.*

*SINKING shriveled on the ground.*
*SWIMMING enters.*
*Looks at her.*
*Walks offstage.*
*Comes back onstage with a sprinkler.*
*Positions it near her.*
*Turns on the water.*
*It mists her lightly.*
*He turns up the water.*
*It drenches her.*
*SWIMMING leaves.*
*We watch the water pour down on her.*
*Soaking her.*
*She grows.*
*Revitalized.*
*She stands.*
*And walks off.*

## SCENE 4

*Lights up.*
*SWIMMING and FLOATING stand around a fish bowl.*
*A dead goldfish floats.*
*They stare.*
*And stare.*
*And stare.*
*They look at each other.*
*Anticipation.*
*SINKING enters.*
*They look at her.*
*She notes their strange position.*
*She looks to the bowl.*
*She spots the floating fish.*
*She runs toward the bowl.*
*She cups the fish with her hands.*
*She places it on the counter top.*
*She gives it tiny compressions.*
*Gentle but frantic.*
*Trying to resuscitate the fish.*
*She fails.*
*She backs away.*
*Stillness.*

**FLOATING**
*Time of death: 5:31 pm*

*SINKING collapses.*

## SCENE 5

*Lights up.*
*A bathroom.*
*Preparation for a fish funeral.*

> SINKING stands near the toilet, dressed in black.
> Maybe she has a veil on.
> SWIMMING enters and takes his place on the opposite side of the bowl.
> FLOATING enters carrying the dead goldfish in a cup of water.
> They all look at each other.
> SWIMMING looks to FLOATING.
> FLOATING haphazardly drops the fish into the toilet bowl.
> It misses the bowl and flops to the ground.
> SWIMMING AND SINKING look at him.

**FLOATING**
Shit. Sorry.

> FLOATING hastily picks up the fish and flings it into the toilet bowl.
> SWIMMING makes a move for the handle.

**SINKING**
WAIT!

> SINKING sinks to the floor.
> She is eye level with the toilet bowl.
> She looks at the floating fish.
> She reaches into the bowl and pets it.
> She moves back.
> She looks up at SWIMMING- giving him the go ahead.
> He flushes the toilet.
> They watch the fish swirl and disappear.
> FLOATING exits.
> A moment.
> SWIMMING exits.
> SINKING puts her head on the toilet bowl.
> Stillness.

## SCENE 6

**FLOATING**
I killed it
The fish
I killed the fish
I killed
I killed
The fish
Drop
A little drop
Just a little drop of dish soap
Drip drop
Drip drop
drippity drop
And it's dead

## SCENE 7

> Lights up.

*FLOATING gutting a fish.*
*The process takes as long as it takes.*
*The smell of fish permeates the space.*
*He fillets the fish meticulously.*
*He transfers the fillets to a searing hot pan.*

*sssss*

*sssssssss*

*SSSSSSSSSSSSSSSSS*

## SCENE 8

*Lights up.*
*SWIMMING sets the table.*
*FLOATING serves the fillets onto plates.*
*He brings them to the table.*
*SINKING enters.*
*An IV bag is attached to her arm.*
*No one seems to acknowledge this.*
*Maybe it has become commonplace.*
*They take their seats.*
*FLOATING shovels a full fillet into his mouth.*
**Chomp.**
**Chomp.**
**Chomp.**
*SWIMMING rips the skin apart with a fork and eats.*
*SINKING stares at her plate.*
*A long moment of stillness.*
*She picks up a fork and knife.*
*She gently cuts the fish.*
*She places a piece in her mouth.*
*She chews.*
*And chews.*
*Laboredly.*
*And swallows.*
*She repeats this process until the fish is gone.*
*She looks at the plate.*
*She gets up from the table and exits.*
*The IV bag drags behind her.*

## SCENE 9

*Lights up.*
*A bedroom.*
*SINKING asleep.*
*An IV bag is still attached to her arm.*
*FLOATING enters.*
*He stands in the doorway.*
*Staring.*
*He slowly approaches the bed.*

> He takes a safety pin out of his pocket.
> He pricks a hole in the IV bag.
> Fluid flows out.
> FLOATING exits.
> We watch the fluid flow until the bag is empty.

## SCENE 10

> Lights up.
> A bathroom.
> SINKING sits in the bathtub.
> The water nearly overflowing.
> SWIMMING sits on the toilet.

**SINKING**
Can I ask you something?

**SWIMMING**
Shoot

**SINKING**
If you could have a superpower–
what would it be?

**SWIMMING**
Um
I don't know
To
to
fly?

**SINKING**
…

**SWIMMING**
What about you?

**SINKING**
To…
swim

> SINKING makes a sudden movement.
> Water spills all over the floor.
> SINKING looks at the floor.
> SWIMMING looks at the floor.
> SWIMMING cups water with his hands.
> Placing it back in the bathtub.
> SINKING looks up at him.
> They look at each other.

## SCENE 11

> Lights up.

> SINKING and SWIMMING sit naked in the bathtub.
> SWIMMING's sopping wet clothes lay on the floor.
> SWIMMING holds her.
> They breathe together.
> He picks up a cup sitting on the side of the tub.
> He scoops up water from the tub.
> He pours it over SINKING's head.
> He repeats the process.
> **Scoop.**
> **Pour.**
> **Scoop.**
> **Pour.**
> **Scoop.**
> **Pour.**
> *Stillness.*

**SINKING**
Thank you

**SWIMMING**
Maybe/
I could-
I could teach you how to swim

> SINKING looks at him.

## SCENE 12

> Lights up.
> A swimming pool.
> SINKING is feverishly stroking.
> SWIMMING stands off to the side observing.
> SINKING exhausts herself.
> She can no longer keep her head above water.
> She sinks.
> And sinks.
> And sinks.
> SWIMMING jumps in.
> He pulls her back to the surface.
> She gasps for air.

**HAAAAAAAH..**
        **HAAAAAAAH.**

                **HAAAAAAhhhhhh.**

> Flailing.

**SWIMMING**
It's the shallow end-
Just stand up

*She stands.*
*Catches her breath.*
*They look at each other.*

## SCENE 13

*Lights up.*
*SINKING lays shriveled in the grass.*
*Stillness.*
*SWIMMING enters.*
*Sprinkler in hand.*

**SINKING**
Don't bother

**SWIMMING**
…

*SWIMMING looks at her.*
*Then exits slowly.*
*A wave of drought.*

## SCENE 14

*SINKING sits alone, naked in a kiddy pool.*
*It is much smaller now.*
*Barely housing her growing body.*
*She swishes the water around with her hands.*

**SINKING**
I'm growing
Splaying out
But I'm not outgrowing this need
This need
to hydrate my cells
I'm quieter about it now
I no longer proclaim my fishy fantasies
But they still permeate my insides
If you gutted me you'd see them entangled in the mess
I convince myself that if I could just submerge my body in enough water
I could swim
I could float
I could-
Maybe I'm delusional
A fish swims
A fish floats
I
I
I
sink
Maybe I'm a pebble
A stone
A piece of rubble

*Plummeting to the seabed*
*I'm not-*
<u>*Not*</u>
**I'm not**
*I'm not a fish*
<small>*I'm not a fish*</small>

## <u>EPILOGUE</u>

>*Lights up.*
>*A body of water.*
>*SWIMMING swims.*
>*FLOATING floats.*
>*SINKING viscously treads water.*
>*She treads.*
>*And treads.*
>*Gasping for air.*
>*Exhausting herself.*
>*She looks for her gills and fins.*
>*Nothing.*
>*Just her painfully human body.*
>*A moment of vigorous treading.*
>*Then surrender.*
>*She sinks.*
>*And sinks.*
>*And sinks.*
>*Until she reaches the bottom.*
>*She looks up at SWIMMING and FLOATING above her.*
>*She looks at the seabed.*
>*She swishes around the sand.*
>*Her hand hits something.*
>*She uncovers it.*
>*An anchor.*
>*Rusted.*
>*A relic.*
>*Of another time.*
>*She pulls it out of the sea bed.*
>*She strokes it.*
>*Gently.*
>*Familiarly.*
>*She curls up into the fetal position.*
>*And pulls it near her.*
>*They become one.*
>*Time and space expand.*
>*They transform into an extension of the seabed.*
>*Stillness.*

**END OF PLAY**

# Jesus Stole My Birth Control (Excerpt)
## Alaina Messineo

**UTERUS**

*A living room.*
*A year without a Santa Claus plays*
*in the background.*
*HER MOM*
*HER SISTER*
*And*
*HER*
*Are decorating a Christmas tree.*
*They speak but cannot hear each other and regard each other as if they were swimming*
*in silence.*

{She's gonna tell Mother. What I did, you hot dog? It's all your fault. Come along. We're not really going to do it, are we, Mrs. Claus? I mean, we're not actually going to disturb her? Oh, she's not serious. We're not really... Are we actually going to see...? Yes. No. Who? Where are we going? Who are we going to see? We're going right to the top, Iggie, my boy. Mrs. C is through fooling around. We're gonna see none other than... Mother Nature. Gosh. I must admit, I was more than a little nervous myself. I'd never met Mother Nature, but I knew she didn't like to be disturbed. As I said, I was pretty nervous myself. I had no idea what to expect of Mother Nature. But frightened as we were, we were that determined... ...that Santa should have his holiday. Oh, so they gave you a hard time, did they, Mrs. Claus? Oh, I'm sure they didn't mean to. Oh, yes, they did. They're nasty little boys, both of them. Ha, ha. Well, I wouldn't say... Oh, I'll straighten them out for you. Oh, yoo-hoo. Children. What is it, Mother dear? Now, Mrs. Claus made a very simple request. Now, you let a little snow fall in Southland... ...and you allow just one nice spring day at the North Pole. All you have to do is compromise. At this time of the year, especially... ...Santa needs some examples of the Christmas spirit... ...and we must set a good example for the people down there to follow. So, boys, please! - I won't do it! - Me, neither. Stop it, stop it! Yes, Mother dear. Hmm. They're really nice boys, Mrs. Claus. Oh, sometimes they bicker, but you'll have no further trouble with them. I do hope Santa enjoys his holiday. How can I ever thank you? Oh, don't mention it. Ta-ta. Well, little girl, I guess you're going to be all right after all.}

                                            **Her Mom**

{It

                                            **Her Sister**

Was

                                            **Her**

Her

                                            **Her Mom**

un

                                            **Her**

Birth

|  |  |
|---|---|
| Control | **Her Sister** |
|  |  |
| Baby | **Her** |
|  |  |
| Cake | **Her Sister** |
|  |  |
| Breathing | **Her** |
|  |  |
|  | **Her Mom** |
| Thanksgiving |  |
|  | **Her Sister** |
| In |  |
| Slowly |  |
|  | **Her Mom** |
| Six |  |
|  | **Her** |
| Li |  |
| Ly |  |
| Li |  |
| Ly |  |
| Lies |  |
| Lilies |  |
|  |  |
| Eye | **Her Sister** |
| Sighs |  |
| For skies |  |
|  | **Her Mom** |
| No orchids |  |
| It was |  |
| Orchids |  |
| I think |  |
|  | **Her** |
| My |  |
| Orange |  |
| Broke |  |
|  | **Her Mom** |
| I |  |
|  | **Her Sister** |
| Can't |  |
| Her |  |
| Breath |  |
|  | **Her Sister** |
| Breathing |  |

|  |  |
|---|---|
| 54321<br>1234567<br>54321 | **Her** |
|  | **Her Sister** |
| Orange<br>Navel | **Her** |
| Orange<br>I | **Her Sister** |
| Waiting | **Her Mom** |
| Uterus | **Her Sister** |
| Shedding<br>The | **Her** |
| Paternity | **Her Sister** |
| Line | **Her** |
| Ing | **Her Sister** |
| Four<br>Set | **Her Mom** |
| Cancer | **Her** |
| Not<br>Lungs<br>But | **Her Sister** |
| Uterus<br>It's<br>In<br>Her | **Her** |
| Uterus | **Her Sister** |
| No | **Her Mom** |
| Her grandma | |

*HER MOM*
*places the star on the tree*

She said

No

Burning

Christmas

Lights

Around

Her

Anymore}

                **Her**

              **Her Mom**

              **Her Sister**

              **Her Mom**

                **Her**

              **Her Sister**

              **Her Mom**

                **Her**

*HER plugs in the tree*
*It lights*
*Up*
*At the same time as the tree lights up* HER GRANDMA *walks on stage*
*The star falls off*
HER MOM *begins to cry and leaves*
HER SISTER *follows her leaving* HER *a "look"*
HER GRANDMA *And makes eye contact with her*
*Blackout*

writing

# tips & prompts

## writing tips from red penguin editors...

*Resist self-editing on a first draft.
*Practice stream of consciousness writing (lose the outline & see what you discover).
*Let the plot develop from what the characters want/need (from eachother and from themselves).
*Stop comparing your practice to others (surrender to what comes naturally to you! If that isn't waking up at 5:30 am- that's okay!)
*Write what **you** want to read!

## writing challenge...

*Write uniterrupted for 10 minutes a day.
*No editing
*No erasing
*Foward moving only!
*See what you have after a month. (And submit it to the next issue of Bloom!)

## writing prompts...

*Write something with no dialogue
*Write something with ONLY dialogue
*Write something that starts with a sound
*Write something that starts with a light
*Write something inspired by a painting
*Write something that uses typography to enhance the storytelling
*Write a multi-media piece (hyperlinks? collage?)
*Write something that uses form as a primary mode of storytelling
*Write something from the perspective of a non-human (an animal? an object? an alien?)
*Write something that focuses on a sensory experience (focus on the visceral rather than cerebral)
*Write something that includes at least 3 moments of physical touch
*Write something with a change of breath

# publishing opportunities

**\*Tradition & Hybrid Publishing Opportunities at Red Penguin Books**
- For full-length manuscripts only
-Go to redpenguinbooks.com/book-publishing or email stephanie@redpenguinbooks.com to find more information!
-Deadline: rolling

**\*The Red Penguin Collection**
-An anthology collection for short form work.
-Each collection focuses on a different theme or genre, ranging from mystery and romance to coming of age stories & social topics.
-Submit up to 5000 words of short stories, essays, plays, or excerpts.
-No cost!
-Go to redpenguinbooks.com/the-red-penguin-collection/ or email thepenguincollection@gmail.com to find more information!
-Deadline: specific to individual anthologies

**\*Bloom- Issue 2**
-Another edition of Bloom, a literary magazine dedicated to the growth of the emerging author.
-Submit up to 1500 words of short stories, essays, plays or excerpts
-No cost!
-Go to redpenguinbook.com/bloom-lit-magazine or email bloomlitmagazine@gmail.com to find more information!
-Deadline: March 15, 2021

# educational opportunities

**Classes With Open Registration:**

*Marketing Your Book with Publisher Stephanie Larkin
*Poetry Workshop with Award-Winning Poet Linda Trott Dickman
*Creative Writing Course with Author Margreit Maitland

**Coming Up Soon:**

*Editing Your Manuscript!

To find more information visit https://redpenguinclasses.com/